HEROES OF
SCOTLAND YARD

by

SAM JACKETT

ILLUSTRATED

THE ADVENTURERS CLUB

LONDON

THE ADVENTURERS CLUB
178-202 Great Portland Street, London, W.1

First published in Great Britain
by Robert Hale Limited

This edition 1966

PRINTED IN GREAT BRITAIN BY
CLARKE, DOBLE AND BRENDON LTD.
CATTEDOWN, PLYMOUTH

CONTENTS

ILLUSTRATIONS

(between pages 96 and 97)

INTRODUCTION

Kicks and Ha'pence

DETECTIVE-SERGEANT RAYMOND PURDY sat at his desk in Chelsea police station typing a report on a criminal investigation he had been making. The telephone rang. He listened carefully, made a quick note, then called to his colleague, Detective-Sergeant John Sandford, to accompany him to the underground station at South Kensington to help him arrest a man they had been seeking.

The telephone call was from Post Office engineers who had, by arrangement with the police, been tapping the telephone of a local woman whose flat had been broken into and robbed some weeks earlier, and who had since been receiving menacing and obscene calls, obviously from the man who had raided her flat.

It was 3 p.m. on a lovely sunny afternoon in July 1959, and the two detectives wasted no time in getting to their car because the Post Office engineers had reported that the man they were seeking for the robbery was at that moment talking to the woman from a telephone kiosk in the underground station. They parked their car, entered the station together, and arrived at the kiosk just as the man was leaving.

They told him who they were, and arrested him. It was quickly and efficiently done. Few people, if any, in the station realized that an arrest had been made, and the man walked quietly with the officers to their car. On reaching the street, however, he suddenly broke free, and bolted. With the detectives on his heels he reached Onslow Square before they overhauled him, and once again took him into custody.

They led him into the hall of a block of flats in the square, and to save any further trouble with the prisoner, decided to ring Chelsea police station to summon transport. Sergeant Purdy stood guard over the man while Sergeant Sandford left to find the flat porter. Almost immediately the prisoner pulled a gun from his pocket, aimed it at Sergeant Purdy, and shot him dead.

Detective-Sergeant Purdy, aged 43, lost his life in the job he idealized—in the Metropolitan Police Force which he had joined twenty years earlier, and which he had served faithfully and well. Guenter Fritz Erwin Podola, aged 30, was hanged for this senseless killing which typifies the hazards of a policeman's life today.

The shooting of Detective-Sergeant Purdy was no isolated incident exemplifying the courage that it takes to be a police-man, and the dangers he faces daily. Only seven months earlier P.C. Reginald Summers, aged 23, was stabbed to death when he was in the act of breaking up a gang fight outside a dance hall in Seven Sisters Road, Holloway. In the course of the convictions that followed it was stated that several members of the gang were "tooled up." Their "tools" included a weighted stick, five choppers, a plasterer's hammer, an air pistol, and a knife.

Such "tools," plus guns—far, far too many guns—plus coshes, plus jemmies, plus iron bars and knuckle dusters are the weapons police officers must be prepared, and courageous enough, to face at any time of any day or night in the never-ending battle against criminals who are more skilled, better organized, and certainly more vicious than ever before.

No policeman's job is safe whether it is among the villains who haunt Soho or patrolling a lonely beat in the heart of the country. Violence lurks in the most unexpected places. On an average in London alone roughly thirty police officers are injured every week in the course of their duties in protecting other people's lives and property. They are the natural enemies of the enemies of society, yet still they get as many kicks as ha'pence.

Too few appreciate the police until they really need them.

When they have been robbed, or attacked, or frightened, or injured in a car crash, then, and only then, do they learn and really appreciate the training, the skill, the kindliness, the understanding, and the all-round ability of the men in blue to cope with any emergency. Fewer still have any idea of their bravery.

It is true that among the 70,000 or so police officers in England and Wales there are some black sheep—men who yield to the temptation of bribery, men who lose their tempers and wield their truncheons or their fists too freely, and men who steal. The temptations and the aggravations are enormous, and it is not surprising that in coping with the dirty work of society some of the dirt rubs off. No one is more anxious to rid the force of these men than the men in the force themselves.

Against the odd officer who succumbs to temptation there are thousands who refuse. A detective-sergeant friend told me this story of an attempt to bribe him. He had been investigating the activities of a criminal who had made a lot of illegal money from gullible members of the public, and when he was convinced he had sufficient evidence to warrant a prosecution, he summoned the man to his office.

Within a few minutes the crook knew that his game was up, and that he faced imprisonment. He left the office, and left behind a suitcase he had been carrying. So the officer called him back. "Here," he said, "you left this." The criminal took the case, placed it on a desk and opened it. It was stuffed full with pound notes. There must have been hundreds of pounds in it. "No," said the crook with a sly wink. "This is not mine. It must be yours."

But the officer did not fall for this subtle, but deliberate attempt at bribery. He kicked the man, and the case, out of the office. Many similar examples are never told. The criminal with experience is far too clever to have witnesses present when he attempts a bribe. And his hatred of the police officer on his trail is such that he is only too happy to try and frame him.

This, with its consequent stream of trumped-up charges, has resulted, particularly in recent times, in far too much uninformed public criticism, and there is no doubt that the investigation of many such complaints has led to a waste of time that has benefited no one but the criminal. The more police there are off the streets and involved in paper work, the more the crook likes it.

And every single case of complaint has to be investigated. I remember on one occasion some years ago I was "arrested" in South London because in reporting a bombing incident some good citizen telephoned the police station and reported me as a "suspicious character." Unaware of this I was telephoning my story when I saw a uniformed, and rather elderly, police-constable waiting outside the telephone box.

As I stepped out he approached, and asked me to accompany him to the station. When I asked why he told me what had happened. On arrival at the station I produced my Scotland Yard and other passes, explained what I had been doing, and the station sergeant was completely satisfied. As I was about to leave, however, this sergeant instructed the P.C. to make a note of my name, and the incident, for record in their official duty book.

I strongly objected to this, and explained that the very nature of my job might lead to similar "arrests" in various areas of London, and I could see no need for such a record to be kept.

"Have you any complaint about your treatment today?" asked the station sergeant. "On the contrary," I replied, "the officer was most courteous, and both he and you could not have been more understanding." "In that case," said the sergeant, "we will forget it." And my name was not recorded.

Curious as to why he wanted to have a record of such a trivial incident in the first place I asked a senior officer at Scotland Yard to explain. The reason, he said, was that, if on reflection I had complained about the arrest then the Yard would have asked the station for their record. And if it had not been recorded there would have been trouble!

Police-officers are a sitting target for malicious complaints, and far too much time is wasted by officers in writing reports on complaints, and then by their senior officers in investigating them. Time which should be spent in trying to reduce the present appalling crime wave. Everyone who has worked closely with the police, as I have, knows the tremendous job they are doing, and the fantastic hours they have to put in because there are not enough of them.

The Metropolitan Police Force is about 2,000 men short. Fewer than 18,000 have the task of protecting eight million Londoners against the gunmen, the cosh men, the burglars, the housebreakers, the petty thieves, and the hundreds of other criminals, men and women, who live by their wits. It is a pretty thin blue line to combat crime figures which are hitting new peaks. The task is enormous and never-ending, and it takes men of courage to face up to it.

Danger may stalk at every corner, and it is natural to fear danger. It stimulates either flight or fight. But you never see a policeman running from a battle. He is trained to the realization that we are dependant on him. Flight is not considered whatever the circumstances, whatever the odds. The Home Office advertising not so long ago for recruits for the police force headed their notice "Could *you* take on this man-sized job?"

A policeman is often very much on his own these days, and we depend upon his zeal, integrity, loyalty and training. As soon as anything unlawful or unusual happens it is he who becomes the man in control. He knows what to do in every sort of emergency, and does not hesitate to hazard his health and his life in safeguarding the lives and property of others.

The records of the Metropolitan Police Force abound with stories of heroism in the efforts of its members to combat criminals who do not hesitate to use the gun or the cosh, on the old or the young, and whose outrageous conduct is an intolerable menace to the safety of the public. Yet, even on occasions when they know the criminal they are seeking carries a gun the Metropolitan Police very, very rarely request to be armed, as they may do.

Yet in 62 of 1,017 cases of robbery in London in 1962 guns were known to have been carried by criminals, compared with

53 in 1961, and 39 in 1960. In a further 49 cases the thieves appeared to have fire-arms. Sir Joseph Simpson, the Metropolitan Police Commissioner, is known to be worried by this disturbing fact, and whenever fire-arms, unlawfully possessed, come into the hands of the police, the fullest possible investigation is made to trace and cut off the source of supply. In his annual report for that year, 1962, Sir Joseph drew attention to the fact that in several offences more than one of the criminals had been armed, a new trend typical of the changing ways of the more vicious type of modern criminal.

Another disturbing fact is that suspects are often arrested in possession of revolvers, but in such circumstances that the only possible charge is of possessing a fire-arm without a certificate. In such cases the Commissioner makes his views quite clear. "In my opinion," he wrote, "this offence which carries a maximum penalty of three months imprisonment and/or £50 fine should be classified as a more serious one with liability to much heavier penalty." Every police-officer in the country will heartily agree.

The last amnesty in this country was in 1961 and it lasted three months. In that period the fantastic total of 11,518 fire-arms and 280,026 rounds of ammunition were surrendered to the Metropolitan and City of London police. Have you a gun in your house now? A relic of the war? If you have it is a potential danger. Every house is vulnerable at some time or other to the petty thief, and if he breaks in and steals it there is little doubt that he can find a ready market for it, even if he does not use it himself.

And the gunmen, like all criminals, plan their attacks where they least expect to see a policeman. Gun, or no gun they still have a healthy respect for an officer's ability to deal with them. This is where the training for the force counts.

Every candidate for the police must be of good character, physically fit, and able to pass a moderate examination. Once accepted he is put on probation for two years, drawing full pay and allowances.

Eleven training centres serve different areas of the country and every man is given instruction in all things a policeman has to know ... what his essential duties are in the event of an air, car, or train crash, a fire, a burglary, a wounding, an attempt at suicide. Everything, in fact, from a domestic squabble to murder.

Experienced police-officers are the instructors, and the student is given practical demonstrations—there are mock courts, mock murders, mock accidents. Off duty he has to keep physically fit and learn the art of self-defence. Judo and swimming are musts.

When the recruit leaves college he returns to his station, and is given a spell of duty, always with an "old hand" so that he can learn the practical side of the work, and gradually get to know the criminal characters on his "manor."

The intake of recruits in the Metropolitan Police Force averages from 1,300 to 1,400 a year, but at the end of 1962 the force was still more than 2,000 men under its authorized strength of 20,160.

Women, too, play an ever increasing role in the prevention and detection of crime. They have the same power and responsibilities as a policeman, and their gallantry has been no less conspicuous. Tradition, and this training, enables the police-officer to face the unexpected moment of peril, and often promotes him by the drama of sudden events to the stature of a hero.

The introduction of the King's Police Medal for Bravery was announced in 1909 by King Edward VII, a few months after one of the most terrifying gun battles in the history of Scotland Yard—a battle in which four people were shot dead and twenty wounded.

It was in the days before criminals used cars, and chasing them was usually either on foot, or by bicycle and tram-car. Three Yard officers who took part in that 1909 gun battle—though they did not have guns—and who showed outstanding bravery were the first recipients of the King's Medal. In 1933 there were instituted two distinct King's Police Medals—"For Gallantry," and "For Distinguished Service."

Today the Queen's Police Medal for Bravery is awarded only posthumously, and gallantry on the part of the police, in common with other citizens, is recognized by the award, in descending order according to the degree of gallantry, of the George Cross, the George Medal, and the British Empire Medal, and so on.

It is fitting that these stories of police gallantry should begin with the gun battle that precipitated the announcement of the King's Police Medal. By no means is every Metropolitan Police hero mentioned, but if these examples help to indicate the debt that is owed to the men who guard our well-being and our homes, we shall be grateful.

CHAPTER ONE

THE RUSSIAN GUNMEN

I T was a typically cold winter's morning. Heavy mist which had smothered the marshland in North London was gradually clearing when just before 9.30 a.m. two men swung briskly along High Road, Tottenham. They turned off by the Old Palace Music Hall into Chesnut Road, walked unhesitatingly past the rear of the police station, and stopped outside a photographers shop window.

It was Saturday, 23 January 1909, and pay day for most businesses. Wages in those days were counted mostly in shillings Trams were a favoured method of transport, and the car had given no indication of ousting the horse. Crime was by no means as highly organized and skilful as it is today.

There was nothing about the two men that sparked any interest that morning. Nothing unusual about them at all except that despite the freezing day they were without overcoats. Certainly there was nothing to indicate that they were about to embark on one of the most terrifying gun battles in the history of London.

It was in this year that Scotland Yard had estimated that roughly 500 Russian revolutionaries were sheltering in London. They met in all districts, in cellars and basements, and in out-of-the-way attics; and quietly, but with vicious determination, prepared their pamphlets and bombs. And when the small groups into which they had formed themselves ran out of money, they robbed.

So the two men, Jacob Lepidus and Paul Hefeldt, stood gazing, hands in pockets, in the photographers shop window.

pretending to admire the pictures of the parents, the sons and daughters, and the newly born.

Lepidus was tall, powerful-looking with broad shoulders, a long sallow face, and curly black hair. Hefeldt was slighter, younger and fair-haired. The latter knew the area well, because he had for a time been employed at the india rubber works of Messrs. Julius Schnurmann whose premises were immediately opposite the photographers shop where they were standing.

Then the moment they were awaiting arrived. A car turned the corner into Chesnut Road, stopped outside the gates of the Schnurmann's works, and Arthur Keyworth, a 17-year-old clerk, stepped out carrying a wages bag. It contained £80, the weekly wages for the firm—£50 in gold, and £30 in silver and bronze.

At the moment that the car stopped Lepidus and Hefeldt sprang into action. They turned from the photographers and darted across the road, Lepidus donning a mask as they ran. Hefeldt barged into the young clerk, knocked him down, held him by the throat, and grabbed the money bag.

Joseph Wilson, the firm's chauffeur, saw what was happening and leapt from his seat to attack the bandit. Seconds later shots were fired, and Wilson, hearing the whine of the bullets in his ear, realized that he was being shot at. He scrambled to his feet and took cover behind the car.

Hefeldt jumped up with the bag, but this time he was felled. Mr. George Smith, a gas stoker, who was passing by, realized it was a hold-up, and struck out at Hefeldt, knocking him down and forcing the money bag from his hand.

Smith heard four shots. Two went through his cap, a third through his coat, and the fourth hit him in the chest and bowled him over. Hefeldt then once more sprang to his feet, hid the bag beneath his jacket, and with his accomplice who had produced the gun, dashed off.

By this time most of the business houses in the street had been alerted by the shots. Workmen inside the factory heard the hulabaloo, opened the gates and streamed out. Officers from the nearby police station ran out and joined them.

One of the clerks from the works saw Wilson still on his back on the ground near Smith who was bleeding badly from his bullet wound. Keyworth was leaning against a post. Wilson, however, was not hurt, and while employees and some of the people in the street took up the chase of the bandits he jumped back into the car where he was joined by Mr. Julius Schnurmann, the head of the firm, and Police Constables Newman and Coombs, and they set off in pursuit.

P.C. Tyler, who had also been alerted by the shots, had already started off on foot.

When the car turned off Chesnut Road into Scales Road the four occupants saw the two bandits standing on the pavement. Both had their revolvers raised and resting on their left arms, and as soon as they saw the car they opened fire.

The first shot missed; the second smashed through the windscreen and hit Wilson, the chauffeur, in the neck; the third smacked into the radiator and brought the car to a halt; and the fourth hit one of the constables in the leg as he was alighting.

At that moment little Ralph Joscelyn, aged 10, excited by the noise of the shots, and the angry shouts of the pursuers, ran from his home into the street to see what was happening. He was shot and died instantly from a bullet through the heart.

The two bandits made off again, heading north parallel with a railway line and the River Lea, across open marshland, and towards the railway.

P.C. Tyler, who was in the vanguard of those chasing by foot, and who knew the area well, saw the obvious route that the gunmen were taking, and made for a short cut to head them off. As he bore in on them from the left a few minutes later he got near enough to shout, and for them to hear, "Come on give in. The game's up."

Hefeldt turned, took deliberate aim, and P.C. Tyler fell dead with bullets through his forehead and throat.

Off went the bandits again, this time across the railway line just in front of a train. They raced towards the River Lea and turned left along the towpath as they reached it. Another constable and a youth who had been gaining on them saw the two gunmen turn by the council swimming bath and raise their revolvers. Both pursuers fell, each with a bullet wound in the leg.

By this time there was a fair crowd of people giving chase trying to keep the gunmen in sight while at the same time keeping far enough away to dodge the murderous bullets.

Hearing the shouts and the shots approaching a Mrs. Green left her cottage by the river just as the two bandits were passing. One of them snatched the cap pinned to her hair to replace the one he had lost in the chase, and in so doing pulled at her hair.

Mrs. Green shrieked so violently that the bandit coldly put his revolver to her head and pulled the trigger. But, fortunately for Mrs. Green, the revolver was empty. Seeing this the second bandit who had gone on ahead took a pot shot at her. Fortunately again for Mrs. Green he missed.

A few minutes later the gunmen passed near a number of men shooting wildfowl. The chasing crowd yelled at them, "Shoot, Shoot," but the sportsmen were unaware of what had happened, and did not understand what they meant. The bandits passed by, and a great chance was lost.

At Chalk Bridge, a footbridge over the water, one of a number of workmen on duty there was quicker to appreciate that something was wrong. He picked up a brick and threw it at the fleeing men. He received in reply a shot which hit him in the leg.

At this point P.C. Williams saw a public telephone, so he broke off the chase and called Superintendent Jenkins at Stoke Newington police station. He told him what had happened, and the course the murderous gunmen were taking. Superintendent Jenkins ordered all available police-officers to take any arms they could find and close in on the marshes.

By this time nearly 100 people were joined in the pursuit, but as soon as anyone got near the two men they turned and fired—and no one had a gun with which to reply.

The bandits reached the Chingford Road area when across a ploughed field they spotted a tram-car approaching from their left. Lapidus and Hefeldt broke through a hedge, ran across the field, and made towards the tram-car which, unfortunately for the driver, stopped at a normal halt at that moment.

Driver Joseph Slow looked from his window and saw two wild-looking men brandishing revolvers. As he made to start again four shots crashed through the windscreen near his head, so he left the controls, dashed up the stairs to the upper deck and lay on the floor.

The bandits boarded the tram-car, and one of them seized Charles Wyatt, the conductor, by the collar, and with a pistol at his head, pushed him through the car to the controls. The three passengers, a woman and her child, and a Mr. Edward Loveday, aged 60, sat motionless with terror.

The gunman ordered Wyatt to drive, and when he protested that he had never driven before, he coolly cocked his revolver, placed it on the back of the frightened conductor's neck, and ordered again, "Drive."

Wyatt set the car in motion just as the first batch of pursuers crossed the field into the road. Seeing that they were continuing the chase one of the bandits moved to the rear of the car, rested his revolver on the control board there, and fired at them at random. More people fell wounded.

Mr. Loveday had by this time recovered something of his composure. He got up from the floor where he had been lying, moved to the front, and started attacking the man who held the gun on Wyatt who was driving. His reward for his courage was a shot in the neck.

The line at this point was single track, and Wyatt had to halt at a loop to let a northbound car go by. The woman and her child took advantage of this moment, and leapt from the tram to safety.

This momentary halt also enabled the pursuers to gain slightly, and a pony and billposters cart with a police-constable on board closed to within twenty yards. The gunman in the rear of the tram-car turned his revolver on them, and the pony fell dead, overturning the cart and shooting the occupants out.

The people in the tram-car which had passed on the loop saw this happen and warned their driver. He quickly reversed his car and joined in the chase, this time with policemen as passengers. These officers, one or two of whom were armed, had fortuitously arrived at that moment following the orders of Superintendent Jenkins.

Wyatt, in the meantime, was driving the bandits as slowly as he dared, but in complete terror. In addition to the guns his great fear was that the driver on the upper deck might unship the electric arm, and bring the car to a standstill. He had little doubt that if this happened he would be killed.

His relief came in a most unexpected manner. As they approached Kites Corner he said, "There is a police station round the corner here." The bandit who was guarding him replied, "You are a liar." Wyatt then retorted, "All right then. I'll drive you there."

For some unknown reason this appeared to convince the man who held the gun on him. He shouted to his accomplice and both jumped off the tram-car and ran off left down St. John's Road.

Here George Conyard, a milkman, had just finished delivering to a house, and was walking back to his cart, when the fleeing men saw him and fired. Conyard fell with bullets in the chest and thigh, and watched helplessly as the gunmen seized his cart, jumped aboard, and whipped the horse to a gallop.

Only a few minutes earlier P.C. Adams had commandeered a private car, and he was riding on the step as they began steadily to overhaul the gunmen. Their effort was foiled when the bandits drew the cart across the road, and blocked it so that the car could not pass.

Taking to their heels again the two men now realized that the chase must be nearing its end. Both had practically run out of ammunition, and they were about spent with exhaustion. They decided to separate.

Hefeldt went over a level crossing to the fields beyond, while Lapidus ran left along Winchester Road, by the Ching brook, and attempted to climb a high fence. He had no strength left to do so, and after a final despairing effort, he turned in terror.

The angry pack of hunters were now at his heels, and they did not stop when he fired two shots in their midst. There was a look of terror in his eyes when suddenly he put the revolver to his head, fired, and fell mortally wounded.

Lapidus reached the fields around Oak Hill, and was fired at by another group of men with shotguns. But the range was too great and the gunman darted across the road to where he saw a number of houses being built. A plasterer who got in his way and tried to stop him was shot down.

Lapidus then side-tracked in an effort to throw his pursuers off the scent, and at Higham's Hill with the crowd still at his heels, ran into the backyard of the end of a row of cottages. Mrs. Eliza Rolstone, a coalman's wife who lived in this cottage, had heard the shots and shouts, and ran to her front gate to see what was happening.

"Get back inside," a P.C. told her. "There is a murderer about."

Mrs. Rolstone obediently turned and re-entered her home. Her heart stopped momentarily, and she froze in terror, for there standing at her back door, still with his gun in his hand, and with his face covered in blood, stood Lapidus.

She opened her mouth to scream when the bandit commanded, "Hush." Then as he moved to enter the house Mrs. Rolstone screamed, "Oh, my children," and rushed for the front door grabbing her younger child in her arms as she fled.

In the cottage the other young child whimpered in a corner as the bandit, now cornered, tried to hide in the chimney. When this failed he poured himself a drink of water, and turning to the child, ordered him to be quiet.

Outside the pursuers pondered on their next step. They knew that one child was still in the house with the gunman, and they feared for the child's life. One man, however, Charles Schafers, did not hesitate. He burst open the front door with a brick, picked up the child, and carried him to safety.

It is believed that at this moment the quarry was slipping upstairs, for a few moments later the people outside saw him through an upstairs window. One or two armed men now with the hunters shattered the window with shot, and were surprised when there was no gunfire in return.

Young P.C. Charles Eagles who had cycled to the cottage, borrowed a double-barrelled breech-loader from a bystander and entered the cottage. He heard Lapidus moving about upstairs, so he left again and went outside looking for a ladder.

He found one nearby and climbed it to a back bedroom window. He could not see the gunman, so he cautiously opened the window—and he saw a dog.

There were no trained police dogs in 1909, but one of the farmers in the chase owned a brown collie which he had sent up the stairs in the hope it would flush the gunman.

P.C. Eagles was trying to get the dog to hide under the bed when Lapidus suddenly appeared at the door, saw the officer, and pointed a revolver at his head. P.C. Eagles was not familiar with the gun he was carrying so he beat a retreat. When he reached the ground he tested the gun and found it would not act!

Detective Charles Dixon had arrived in the meantime, and he carried a revolver. P.C. Eagles borrowed it, once more entered the cottage and with the detective by his side started mounting the stairs.

When they had got about three stairs up they saw a reflection of the gunman's feet under the door. P.C. Eagles fired two shots at the door panels, but they appeared to have no effect.

The door gradually opened and there was Lapidus, his revolver in his left hand, pointing down the stairs towards the two officers.

Here, in P.C. Eagles's own words, "I fired again at the man.

He threw his arms in the air, staggered, and fell on the bed. I had fired again just before he staggered. I rushed in and took the revolver from his left hand."

At the inquest which followed Dr. Allcock said Lapidus had a wound on the right temple, but there was no singeing of the hair, or powder marks around it—which might have been expected if Lapidus shot himself.

P.C. Eagles, who was recalled to give evidence on this point, said he heard no other shots but his own fired. When, however, he was handed a bullet, and asked if it was the same size as those he had used, he replied, "No, mine were four times as big." The bullet he was handed was that which had been taken from the head of the dead man.

The jury, in recording a verdict of *felo-de-se*, specially commended P.C.s Tyler, Eagles and Newman, and Detective Dixon.

There was loud applause in Court when the Coroner said, "On Saturday walking through Tottenham one was exposed to as much danger as if a war was going on. This terrible state of affairs must be stopped."

Paul Hefeldt died in hospital about a fortnight later, and thus ended the lives of two men who showed no sanctity for life in their desperate gun battle which lasted for nearly three hours, and zig-zagged across five miles of North London.

Twenty people were shot, four fatally, in their mad bid for freedom. Later the police estimated that each man had carried about 100 cartridges with his six-chambered Browning revolver.

There is little doubt that the bravery shown by the police in this gun battle, and the way, though unarmed, they stuck close to the trail of the murderers, was the deciding factor which caused King Edward VII to announce six months later the institution of the King's Police Medal for Gallantry.

Detective Dixon, later promoted Detective-Sergeant, and P.C.s Eagles and Newman were the first recipients.

There were questions in the House of Commons about what was being done for the widow of the P.C. who had been killed in the execution of his duty, and Mr. Herbert Gladstone, the Home Secretary, announced that the maximum pension laid down for the widow was £15 a year, plus £2 10s. for each child.

The public, however, responded generously to an appeal for P.C. Tyler's dependants, and the others who had been killed and wounded were not forgotten.

CHAPTER TWO

MAYFAIR BATTLE

How long would that gun battle of North London have lasted today? Time changed the methods of criminals, and of the police. Both raced for supremacy; speed became the vital factor in villainy as well as in detection and apprehension.

Criminals stole fast cars for their smash-and-grab raids, their ambushes of wage-carrying vehicles, and for speedy departure from gun hold-ups. Scotland Yard bought faster cars, and opened a school for drivers to be specially trained in the technique of chasing and stopping bandits.

Business houses were given instructions in security measures they could take, and the old method, so advantageous to the robbers, of collecting or taking money to the bank on the same day and at the same time every week was stopped by most companies.

Members of the public were appealed to to help if they saw any suspicious action, and the introduction of the 999 call, with its instant connection to the Yard's Information Room, brought tremendous response.

When the trams and the horses gradually disappeared, and heavy car traffic started impeding police cars getting to the scene of the crime the Yard introduced cars on permanent patrol in strategic areas. These are in constant radio contact with the Information Room and the nearest car can be directed in a matter of seconds to the scene of any criminal activity.

When the bandits learned, to their cost, of this move, they started using two, or even three cars, for a smash-and-grab, or a hold-up. The first would be used for the actual robbery and getaway, and this car they realized would be seen, described, and probably the number taken and given to the police in a matter of minutes. So they parked a second car not far away, but out of sight of the point of robbery and transferred to it. And if they thought this move had been spotted by any inquisitive bystander they would have a third, further away, to be used if necessary.

This was the state of the battle between the Yard and the criminal when, forty-six years after the gun fight in High Road, Tottenham, there was another between gunmen and police through the streets of London. In this instance, as will be seen, time had vastly changed the method of operation.

It had changed the way the bandits worked, and the way the police got on their trail. One thing that remained constant was the tenacity and supreme courage of the unarmed police who faced the bullets until they got their man.

On 10 October 1955, just before 12.30 on a rather pleasant sunlit afternoon two men got out of a car in Hogarth Place, Earl's Court, and walked casually into the Jeweller's shop of H. R. Drew & Son, Ltd. Once inside there was nothing casual about their movements.

The first man drew a .38 revolver from his pocket and said to the three men inside, "This is a hold-up. Don't move or touch the telephone or I'll plug you." The second man closed and bolted the shop door. Mr. H. R. Drew, aged 67, proprietor of the business, Mr. E. Caffel, aged 32, the manager, and Mr. L. Williams a 22-year-old assistant, had no doubt that the intruders meant business.

Mr. Williams was sitting on a chair behind the counter and one of the bandits motioned to him to join the other men. Because he hesitated, and did not move immediately, he was hit over the head with the butt of a revolver.

The gunman then forced Mr. Drew to unlock one of the steel doors of an inner compartment to the safe which contained a considerable amount of jewellery, including gold and diamonds, lying loose on a shelf.

One of the men, who wore a brown leather glove on his left

hand, evidently to prevent leaving fingerprints, scooped jewels from the shelf and stuffed them into his pocket, meanwhile keeping the staff of the shop covered with the gun held in his right hand.

After the raid had been in progress about three minutes there was an unexpected interruption, and one, which for some inexplicable reason, the raiders had not taken into consideration.

Two girls, Miss Marion Ford, aged 17, of Forest Gate, and Miss Sheila Stewartson. aged 18, of Loughton, Essex, who worked at nearby Earl's Court Station were taking a lunch time stroll when Miss Ford decided to have her watch, which had been giving trouble, repaired.

They decided to have this done at Drews. When they tried the door of the shop they were surprised to find that it was locked. One thought it was closed for lunch, but the other was certain that it never closed at that period.

They rattled the door and knocked. Nothing happened so they peered through the window. At that moment one of the gunmen wheeled round, and both girls saw the gun in his hand. They screamed and ran into a butcher's shop next door to tell their story and raise the alarm.

The bandit nearest the door of the shop, who appeared to be the more nervous of the two, had seen the girls and he said to his companion, "Look out, we've been spotted."

Both men then looked out of the window and though they saw no sign of any alarm, they guessed what might be happening, and walked quietly from the shop.

Mr. Caffel sprang for the telephone and dialled 999 as Mr. Drew and his assistant ran to the window and saw the two bandits cross the road and leap into a grey saloon car which immediately made off.

Mr. Drew spotted the number of the car, and shouted it to Mr. Caffel who was at that moment reporting the hold-up to the Information Room at Scotland Yard, and who repeated the number to the officer on duty. Within two seconds all patrol cars cruising around Chelsea, Kensington, Westminster and further afield had been given a description of the car, its index number, and the fact that it had three men in it two of whom were certainly armed.

At 12.35 as the bandits', car turned into Cromwell Road two area patrol cars saw it and took up the chase. At Queen's Gate a third police car joined in but the traffic was thick and they made little headway.

Detective-Sergeant Albert Eric Chambers, of Scotland Yard's Flying Squad, was in a squad car with Detective-Sergeant Ernest Cooke, and Police-Constable Donald Cameron driving, going south across the Serpentine Bridge, Hyde Park, when they received the radio message about the hold-up.

Soon aferwards they saw the fugitive car coming towards them. P.C. Cameron swung the police car around, gave chase, and caught up with the fleeing grey saloon at a traffic block near Victoria Gate.

Both cars were forced to a halt, and although unarmed and fully aware that the bandits had guns Sergeant Chambers leapt from one side of the police car and Sergeant Cooke from the other, and both raced on foot towards the bandits' car.

Sergeant Cooke reached the offside of the wanted car just as the traffic was about to be released through the Gate. He saw that the driver's window was down, so he reached for the steering wheel hoping to swing the car to the left. At that moment the driver accelerated and swung the car violently to the right, throwing Sergeant Cook off balance and into the roadway in the path of oncoming vehicles.

Sergeant Chambers quickly returned to the police car, and P.C. Cameron immediately drove after the criminals, leaving a very angry and frustrated colleague in the roadway.

All this time messages were being relayed back to the Information Room at the Yard indicating how close the pursuers were to the bandits, and particularly the course they were taking so that other patrol cars could be directed in the hope of heading them off.

The bandits car headed east along North Carriageway to Marble Arch, and at times reached a speed of 70 miles per hour. Then it went down East Carriageway, through Grosvenor Gate into Park Lane and Stanhope Gate. P.C. Cameron, driving with exceptional skill, kept it in view all the way, and at Stanhope Gate the cars were only ten to fifteen yards apart.

At this point one of the bandits, sitting in the front passenger seat, leaned through the window of the stolen car and fired two shots at the police car; the first apparently missed, but the second made a hole in the centre of the windscreen and caused extensive cracking which blurred the officer's view. The flying glass also cut P.C. Cameron about the hands which started to bleed badly.

Both officers heard the "ping" as the bullet whistled past them, and the hole it caused was about nine inches in diameter slightly to the right of the midline of the windscreen. What bothered them most at this moment, however, was that one side of the windscreen was completely shattered and frosted, and it was only with great difficulty that they could see where they were going.

Appreciating the difficulty of his colleague, Detective-Sergeant Chambers climbed from the rear seat of the squad car to the front, and helped P.C. Cameron clear some of the glass away—to make a hole large enough for them to see through and continue the chase. Both men realized that not only were the bandits armed but that one at least was prepared to use his gun to prevent capture. This knowledge by no means deterred them, and though handicapped by the smashed windscreen, P.C. Cameron kept his car on the tail of that of the bandits.

Pursued and pursuers turned from Stanhope Gate into South Audley Street and here it was that the officers learned that more than one of the bandits was prepared to shoot it out. The criminal in the rear passenger seat of the runaway car leaned out of the near side window and took careful aim at them with his pistol. They saw the flash and heard the bang, but so far as they knew neither they nor the car was hit.

Both officers remained calm and unperturbed. They fully realized the danger, but there was no thought of abandoning the chase, and they were still close behind the fugitives when they turned into Curzon Street. And here it was, for the first time, that the driver of the bandit's car, who had shown great skill and daring, erred.

Heavy traffic forced him over to the wrong side of the road, and as he swerved from side to side trying to dodge the cars, vans and lorries, he hit the offside door of a chauffeur-driven car which had just driven out of Chesterfield Street. He reversed immediately but crashed into a taxi and was forced to stop.

Scores of people in and around Curzon Street heard the crashes of the collisions and stopped and turned to look. What they saw within the next few minutes was reminiscent of an old style Chicago gangster film with guns firing, men shouting, police car bells ringing, and police cars screeching to a halt.

They saw the three bandits leap from their car, one of them brandishing a .38 revolver, and as the fugitives fled some of the more daring spectators started to give chase. Two of the criminals ran along Hertford Street, and the third, the driver, who was not seen again by the police that day, bolted along Curzon Street.

Sergeant Chambers and P.C. Cameron who were immediately behind the bandits' car saw them throw away two corduroy caps and started to give chase on foot—Chambers after the two men along Hertford Street and Cameron after the man in Curzon Street. So dense was the traffic that after about fifty yards P.C. Cameron lost sight of his man so he decided to return to his Squad car to maintain wireless communication with the Information Room at Scotland Yard.

On the way back he examined the bandits' car and found on the floor of the front passenger seat a flat square box which contained a false moustache. He also found two ear-rings and an expanding gold bracelet which had been stolen from the jewellers.

He picked up the two caps which had been thrown away by the bandits and someone in the crowd handed him a black Homburg hat which he said the third man had discarded.

When he returned to his own car he saw a bullet mark on the bonnet. The bandits had scored two hits in the three shots they fired during the chase! And suddenly he remembered having seen the driver of the stolen car before. He was a man he helped two detectives to arrest in November 1952.

In the meantime Sergeant Chambers continued with the chase, but he too was hampered by the traffic and by the milling crowd. He ran along Hertford Street and turned left towards Shepherd Market when he lost sight of them in the chaos. Men and women were running in all directions, many towards telephones to dial 999; others in the belief that they were joining in the chase. There were shouts of, "There they are," and "Stop that man," coming from all directions.

A housekeeper in Charles Street went to answer her front door bell and saw the gunman bandit only a few yards away. He started shooting a second later—two shots as if to clear a way, and she saw an officer fall wounded. She ran back upstairs to summon a doctor to go to his aid.

As Sergeant Chambers continued with his hunt for the bandits he was joined by P.C. David Evans Wood, who was on beat duty in Curzon Street and had seen the criminals leave their car, and P.C. George William Karn who was on motor cycle patrol at the corner of Hertford Street and Curzon Street when he heard shots fired.

Sergeant Chambers turned right at Charles Street and heard a shot fired at the Berkeley Square end. He headed that way and saw P.C. Karn board a lorry. He jumped on too but they could not get far because of the traffic, so they both abandoned it and ran in the direction of people shouting, "There he is," "There he goes."

There is no doubt that at this stage the gunman lost his head completely. He was shooting at random. He was very, very dangerous. He jumped on the running board of a lorry which had already been forced to a standstill by traffic, pushed his gun through the window at the driver and ordered, "Move on."

The driver and his mate saw that the man was red in the face and perspiration was pouring from him. They saw his look of wild determination too, and the lorry moved a yard or so before again being forced to a halt. Then, surprisingly, the gunman ordered, "Get out." The driver did so, but his mate stayed on and saw the gunman jump off and run towards Berkeley Square. Just as he did so two uniformed officers ran towards the lorry, the driver re-mounted, the officers joined him, and they tried to chase the man. After ten yards traffic again brought them to a standstill.

The two officers, P.C.s Wood and Karn, carried on on foot, and saw ahead of them the bandit jump on the nearside running board of a taxi which was at the junction of Queen Street and Charles Street.

As the driver of the taxi turned and said, "I'm engaged," he saw the gun pointing at him. "Keep moving," ordered the gunman, and at that moment his woman passenger on her way to lunch in Park Lane, spotted the gun and screamed. Traffic was still so thick that the taxi could make little headway and the woman pleaded with the gunman, who had now joined her in the passengers seat, "Please let me get out." Disturbed by her screams the gunman ordered her to do so. Thankfully, though tearfully, she did so, and a second or so later was followed by the gunman who had observed a police officer catching up with the vehicle on foot.

Ignoring the threats, the shots, and the danger, the police were sticking to this, the most dangerous, of the criminal trio. P.C. Karn got to within three yards of him before the bandit turned, pointed his .38 and fired. The shot missed and P.C. Karn took off his crash helmet, hurled it at the man, hitting him in the back of the neck as he fled.

Seconds later, P.C. Karn again saw the gunman, this time running towards him and being hotly chased by P.C. Wood. As the bandit ran past him he again threw his helmet and this time struck him on the face whereupon the bandit turned and fired another shot. This slowed him up, and almost immediately P.C. Wood caught up with him and grabbed him by the lapel of his jacket. As he did so the man deliberately raised his revolver and fired at P.C. Wood who fell forward on his face, shot in the right leg.

Immediately after this shot the gunman ran into the path of

Sergeant Chambers. He was running on the pavement and the sergeant in the roadway with a row of parked cars between them. Both were running in the same westerly direction, almost abreast.

After a moment the bandit spotted the officer, saw how close he was, and fired at him over the roofs of the parked cars. As far as the officer could tell the bullet did not hit him. The reason why the officer could not be certain about this will be understood later.

Both men ran on like this for a matter of about twenty to thirty yards until Sergeant Chambers spotted a gap between the cars and ran through and on to the pavement. Once again he saw the revolver raised, pointed at him and fired but again the officer did not feel anything and could not be certain whether it hit him or not.

His whole mind, every nerve in his body, was concentrating on one thing and one thing only . . . of getting his hands on the gunman. Sergeant Chambers, 39 years old, weighing nearly 17 stone, and with 18 years experience in the force, did not know the meaning of the word fear.

In another pace or two he was on top of the bandit. He dived forwards, caught the man's ankle, and both fell flat on the pavement. The officer pulled himself up on the man's legs, twisted the revolver from his hand, and with the aid of P.C. Karn and some civilians who arrived simultaneously, soon overpowered him.

They hauled the gunman to his feet and the sergeant and P.C. Karn took him into a hall in Charles Street. They sat him on a chair and P.C. Karn remained on guard while Sergeant Chambers went to telephone for assistance. As he lifted the telephone he saw blood on his hand and then realized, for the first time, that he had a bullet hole in his arm. So tense, so exciting were the moments of this chase, that the officer could not say which of the shots fired at him had caused the wound. Neither did he realize until later that there were three bullet holes in the jacket he was wearing!

The second bandit was caught without a struggle. The third

got clean away but was arrested two days later in a hotel where he had been hiding.

When this man was shown a statement that had been made by the man who did the shooting he exclaimed, "He's singing like a canary. I was there. I was driving. I did not shoot anyone. I have got no time for violence."

It emerged later that two of this gang of three had been released from Dartmoor only three weeks before the raid on the jeweller's shop, and all three had a string of previous convictions. They all met and lived together in Finsbury Park planning "some jobs to do."

About a week before the raid on the jewellers they stole a Rover car in Russell Square, and altered the letters on the index plates from PXB to PXP by cutting out part of the last letter. Two of them bought revolvers and ammunition for £6 in a Soho club, and on the day before the raid changed their address to a room flat at Redfern Road, off the Harrow Road. On the morning of the raid they got into the car, two of them with fully loaded revolvers, looking for a place to "stick-up."

In the flat which they had occupied the police later found dum-dum bullets—bullets with their noses split by a penknife—and bullets which have been ruled contrary to international warfare.

Sentences totalling forty-two years were imposed on the three men. The man who did the shooting in Curzon Street, a 25-year-old labourer, got twenty years, and the other gunman, a 22-year-old waiter, twelve years. The driver, aged 29, a machinist, received ten years.

At the start of his summing up to the Jury, the Lord Chief Justice (then Lord Goddard) said, "I am sure you will agree with me when I say the most satisfactory feature of this case has been the courage and devotion to duty shown by all the police-officers concerned, which seems to me to be most praiseworthy."

And after sentencing the prisoners the Lord Chief Justice called the five police-officers before him and said, "I have asked you men to parade in front of me to give you the thanks of the community for your gallant and devoted sense of duty on the day in question. It takes courage of no mean order to run up and tackle desperate criminals who are in possession of firearms. The Metropolitan Police Force has reason to be proud of you and, as I say again, I thank you on behalf of the community and commend you for your gallantry."

Later it was announced that Detective-Sergeant Chambers, P.C. Wood, and P.C. Karn had each been awarded the George Medal for their bravery; Driver P.C. Cameron the British Empire Medal, and Detective-Sergeant Cooke the Queens commendation for brave conduct. The last named, incidentally, commandeered a private car after he had been thrown from the bandits' car, and followed his colleagues as fast as he could.

So rapid were the events, however, that by the time he arrived at Charles Street the gunman had been arrested. Altogether, from the moment they bolted from the jeweller's shop, this gun battle had lasted roughly twenty minutes—twenty minutes as compared with the three hours it took to capture the gunmen of Tottenham High Road in 1909.

As so aptly put by Lord Goddard to the Jury, "Fifteen or twenty years ago they might have got away with it, but nowadays we owe a lot to the incredible speed with which the police can work."

Four years after this Mayfair shooting Sergeant Chambers was one of the officers chosen to effect the arrest of Podola, the man who murdered P.C. Purdy. He it was, in fact, who burst open the hotel door where the gunman was hiding, and led his colleagues in to the capture.

His resignation from the Metropolitan Police Force in May 1962, after 25 years of most distinguished service, was a sad loss to the force, and particularly to the Flying Squad, which he had served so bravely.

CHAPTER THREE

BANK DECOY

WHEN known dangers have had to be faced Scotland Yard has never wanted in volunteers. On the contrary there are men —and women—in the force who have braved certain serious injury with the sole object of ensuring that criminals would be caught and punished.

Now and again through what is officially described as "information received" the Yard learn of a planned attack, and the task of the officers then is to outwit the gang; ideally to prevent the crime but by such methods that the perpetrators are caught with sufficient evidence to ensure a conviction.

Mostly the "information received" comes from "snouts," underworld men and women who mix with the gangs and learn, by devious means, of their plans. They pass on this information to an officer with whom they have had previous dealings, always, of course, for a cash reward.

Occasionally C.I.D. officers themselves undertake the risky job of pretending to be crooked, and ready to join in any planned mischief.

This happened some time ago when there was a violent outbreak of lunch-time office breakings in the West End. During the lunch-hour thieves entered dozens of offices, and stole cash and everything else of value they could lay their hands on.

Suspicion eventually centred on four known criminals who were seen to meet in a public house shortly after opening time every day, and enjoy themselves with beer and darts until just after noon.

It was decided to plant a young C.I.D. officer, unknown to

them, in the pub to try and learn more about them, but particularly, if possible, to join them. Day after day he drank his beer quietly and alone. The gang ignored him, and he took little interest in them except for an occasional nod of appreciation for a good dart throw.

Then one day the gang arrived one short. They asked the officer to make up a four at darts. He agreed, and in response to their queries gave the impression that he was out of luck, out of work, and ready for any job—with an emphasis on the *any*.

Before long the leader had taken him into his confidence. They could give him a job. It would last an hour. It was an easy job. All he had to do was wait outside an office while they broke in, and raise the alarm if he saw anyone else about to enter the office, or if any "coppers" approached.

The young C.I.D. officer agreed. Separately the four men left the public house and made their different ways to the office earmarked for robbery. The only man followed was the C.I.D. officer—by another C.I.D. officer to whom he whispered the office address as they passed.

Within a few minutes of the gang having broken into the office they were all arrested in the act. Still wondering, possibly, what happened to the new and fourth member of their gang.

There was an element of danger in that job, but not nearly as much as that which faced Flying Squad Detective-Sergeant William Deans, and which had its sequel at the Old Bailey when six members of a most vicious gang were sentenced to a total of twenty-nine years penal servitude.

Immediately after he had imposed those sentences Lord Goddard, then the Lord Chief Justice, turned his attention to the well of the court and ordered, "Stand up, Detective-Sergeant Deans."

Deans, a slight man, and rather below the average height for a police-officer, stood to attention. All eyes focussed on him as the Lord Chief Justice said:

"The country—and London in particular—are most indebted to you for the extraordinary courage and devotion to duty you have shown in this case. You have added lustre to the already great record of the force to which you belong. I shall make it my duty to call the attention of the Secretary of State to your most commendable conduct."

No man more fittingly deserved this tribute. It took cool, calculated courage and nerves of steel to do what he did— to act as decoy for the gang the members of which he knew full well would show him no mercy.

It had come to the ears of the Flying Squad that this gang of villains were showing particular interest in the movements of a Mr. Snell, cashier of the Midland Bank in Kentish Town. The Yard men had an informant close to one or two members of the gang, and knew it was their intention to waylay the cashier on his way home one evening, attack him, steal the keys of the bank, and rob it.

It was learned that, for some time early in 1947, members of this gang had been watching and following the bank official in order to become conversant with his habits and movements from the time he left the bank until he reached his home in Westbury Road, Finchley.

They had decided exactly where they would make the attack, and how they would dispose of the bank cashier during the time they were robbing the bank. It was known, too, that they planned to split up, one section waylaying the official while the others remained in the vicinity of the bank.

The problem facing the Yard was to catch them—all of them—and catch them in the act. They knew that the greatest discretion would have to be used, for the leaders of these crooks were experienced men, men who could "smell a detective," and men who would flee at the slightest suspicion that all was not well with their plans.

Careful, and secret, inquiries made it quite clear that the gang was six strong, and they would not hesitate to use violence to enforce their plans.

It was a tricky problem to decide how to trap, catch and convict such experienced villains. It would be hopeless to have detectives follow the bank cashier home. The gang would spot that immediately. An ambush was out of the question as that would result in the capture of only those members of the gang who were going to attack the cashier.

Detective-Superintendent George Hatherill, later Commander, and head of the detectives at Scotland Yard, was put in over-all charge, and he set about the task of organizing a plan which had as its object the capture of all six members of this most dangerous company of young desperadoes.

After conferring with the Chief Investigating Officer of the Midland Bank it was decided that it was impracticable for the police to utilize the services of the unsuspecting bank official. He had been seen by detectives, without him realizing who they were, and it was decided that he should not be subjected to physical violence such as that likely to be used by the gang.

It was decided to use a police-officer, and it was at this stage of the proceedings that Detective-Sergeant Deans came into the picture. He was similar in stature and appearance to Mr. Snell, the bank official, and it was thought that he could easily pass for him.

He was told the full story, and the fact that he would almost certainly encounter extreme violence was not disguised from him, but he immediately volunteered. And so, with Sergeant Deans to act as bait, the plans were laid in the utmost secrecy.

Sergeant Deans at first familiarized himself with the route home invariably taken by the bank official. This meant a rail journey from Kentish Town to Woodside Park station, then a walk of about 400 yards down a narrow footpath to Holden Road, and then uphill to Argyle Road which leads into Westbury Road.

He was told that the criminals planned to seize him at the junction of Holden Road and the footpath, bind him with rope and adhesive plaster, place him in a van, rob him of the bank keys, and hold him prisoner while the keys were delivered to the rest of the gang whose job it was to enter the bank. Then at least four members of the gang were to board the van which was to be driven to the suburbs of Chingford where he would be dumped in a lane.

When the informant was seen by the police again he was emphatic on two vital points—(1) That the raid would take place on a Friday evening, and (2) That he would be able to give the officers twenty-four hours notice of it.

This man certainly knew the answers to all the questions. He knew, for example, that the leader of the gang had taken into account the fact that the bank official's family would be disturbed if he did not arrive home at the usual hour, so, to allay their suspicions, one of the gang would telephone his home and say he had been detained on business.

It was a daring, cunning plan, and Sergeant Deans had no doubt that the men organizing it were vicious and determined. But he had no qualms.

One vital point at this stage of the inquiry was that there should be no leakage of the Yard's plans, and that as few people as possible should know of their plot to use the sergeant as a decoy.

So it was arranged that on the day they learned the robbery was to take place Mr. Snell would be called to the Bank's Head Office on fictitious business at midday. The plan would then be disclosed to him, and he would be asked to loan Sergeant Deans his hat and coat. Then, after lunch, Sergeant Deans, dressed in Mr. Snell's clothing, would return to the bank, preceded by an inspector who would tell the Bank Manager what was happening, and set his mind at rest.

As a further precaution Sergeant Deans was to carry correspondence in the name of Snell, two bunches of bank keys, four marked one pound notes, one marked ten shilling note, and four marked half-crowns, a total of £5.

It was anticipated that not only would he be attacked, but that he would be searched, and the letters would, it was hoped, convince the gang that they had got the right man. And it was thought that if they took his cash—and no one had any doubt that they would—it would help in evidence towards their conviction. Just how wise these precautions were will be shown.

At a conference at the Yard Detective-Inspector Crawford was put in charge of a team of officers deputed to take the necessary action and having been over and checked the route, it was decided that they would have to allow Sergeant Deans to continue the deception until such time as the whole gang could be rounded up—when he was gagged and bound and the van guarded by some members of the gang, and until the rest had started their raid on the bank.

Then groups of officers who would be watching the van and the bank would pounce at a given signal and arrest the lot.

This meant, of course, that the Flying Squad sergeant would have to submit to the attack, the binding and gagging, the dumping in the van, and the questionable company of unquestionably armed villains. And he could expect no aid from his colleagues until the van was driven back to the bank and the six desperadoes were together again. Still he did not hesitate.

Arrangements were made for police observation to be kept from a house at Holden Road, Finchley, overlooking the expected point of the attack. There was a telephone in the house and contact could be made immediately with the main group of officers who would be centred at Camden Section House.

On Thursday, 6 February, the informant rang to say that the gang had arranged for the robbery to take place the following day. On Friday the Yard's plans were put into effect—and that afternoon Sergeant Deans returned to the bank in the place of Mr. Snell. And at 5.10 p.m. that winter's evening, the sergeant, father of two children, locked up the bank and set off in the blackout on the regular route that Mr. Snell took to his home.

He had told his wife that he might be a little late home that evening as he "had a bit of a job" to do. She had no idea of the perilous nature of that job.

Soon after he started off along the Kentish Town Road he had the feeling that he was being followed. He got to Holden Road, and there was the van. It was all set. Then, just as the gang were preparing to attack him, a uniformed officer who knew nothing of the plans of the gang or the Yard, happened to ride past on his bicycle. This so alarmed the gang that they held their hands, and Sergeant Deans was allowed to pass unmolested. Later that evening the van was seen back in the Kentish Town neighbourhood.

On Thursday, 13 February, the informant again contacted the police and said the robbery would take place the following day. And on Friday, the 14th, the Yard again put their plans into operation, with the added precaution that Sergeant Deans would, if unmolested, proceed to and enter Mr. Snell's home in case he was followed.

Once again he took the lonely, frightening walk, and this time he again knew he was being followed but, for some reason unknown, the gang declined to attack. Something somewhere along the line had upset, or scared, them, and the officer once again reached the home of the cashier unharmed.

On the third Friday, the 21st, Deans went through the same routine. It was a bitterly cold day and there was snow on the ground, but once again soon after leaving the bank he was aware he was being followed.

As he entered Kentish Town station he took a fleeting glance round and spotted another member of the gang. This, he thought to himself, is the night. So did other officers who were hidden along the route for they had seen that one of the gang was carrying something that looked ominously like a weapon in his hand.

As Sergeant Deans left the train at Woodside Park he spotted a third member of the gang—and it was at this moment that any hope or fear he had that there would be no attack fled. He knew colleagues were about, but he knew too that they could and would not come to his aid until after he had been attacked and kidnapped.

So quietly he walked on through the dark streets, forcing himself not to turn round, forcing himself to concentrate on not giving the slightest indication that he was aware that in a matter of minutes the gang would set on him.

When he reached Holden Road he saw a green van standing under a railway bridge. He crossed the road and had just entered the rarely used footpath when he heard footsteps behind him and a voice say, "Right."

At that same moment he received a heavy blow on the head which removed his hat which had been lined to give him some protection, and he fell to the ground. As he lay there he received other heavy blows with a weapon before he became unconscious.

He was picked up by two of the gang and thrown into the back of the van. Adhesive plaster was placed over his lips and his own scarf was tied about his eyes. His keys, money, and watch were taken from him.

Then the van started off, and in a few moments Deans groaned. Someone stuck something hard into his right side and said, "This is a stick-up. Keep y'r —— mouth shut, or it's your lot."

The van travelled on and after a few more minutes one of the gang asked, "Are you sure it's the right bloke?" Another voice replied, "He's the geezer all right. He's got the keys in his pocket."

Deans next heard a voice ask, "Are you sure he's all right?" Someone then felt his pulse and his heartbeats, and then forced one of his eyes open and shone a light on it.

A voice said, "He looks bad; you hit him too hard, Jim." Another man replied, "It doesn't matter—no one saw us do it."

The van cruised around for an hour with Deans bound and gagged, and suffering from concussion. He had no idea where they went, and the bandits were for the most part silent. Fortunately for him they never guessed that he was a police-officer. The letters and the bank keys that he carried had played a vital part in the deception.

Then after an hour, an hour of indescribable anxiety, the van stopped. One of the gang lifted Deans on to his shoulder and carried him, still bound and gagged, a short distance before flinging him face downwards into a pile of snow.

This, although Deans was not aware of it, was at East Barnet. He lost consciousness again, but after a time came to. He pulled the scarf from his mouth, kicked his ankles free, and, despite his condition, staggered to a house fifty yards away. Here, the occupier, gave him first aid, and called the Divisional Surgeon who found him suffering from concussion, and from exposure to severe cold.

This actual attack on Sergeant Deans was seen by Detective-Inspector Crawford and Woman P.C. Sherwin, and the former alerted the waiting officers at Camden Section House who went to pre-arranged points of observation to await developments.

It had already been decided not to attempt to follow the van, but to await its arrival in the Camden Town area. Here, however, unfortunately for the police, the gang's plans went astray, for the vehicle, a hired one, developed engine trouble *en route* to Camden Town with the result that three men left the vehicle and made their way to the bank by bus and taxi.

Detective-Inspector Crawford rushed to Kentish Town and joined other officers who were watching the bank. When the van failed to appear the Yard men became increasingly anxious as to the fate of Sergeant Deans, but it was not until 7.10 p.m., forty minutes after their expected time of arrival, that there was any action from the raiders.

One of them was seen to approach the bank. All he saw was what he thought were a courting couple walking arm-in-arm, but they were a detective and a woman detective; and as soon as he put a key in the door of the bank he was arrested, and Inspector Crawford tried to force from him the whereabouts of Sergeant Deans.

The prisoner was in possession of the two bunches of bank keys and Sergeant Deans's wrist watch. He was interrogated in a police van, and revealed that the van had broken down, but professed that he did not know where it was or what had happened to Sergeant Deans.

Knowing that the gang came from the Walthamstow district Inspector Crawford sent out a wireless message for all available Flying Squad officers to join him at Hackney police station where he made intensive inquiries as to the whereabouts of Sergeant Deans.

Once he learned what had happened to the sergeant the inspector so ably dealt with the prisoner in his hands that by midnight three others had been arrested, the van had been traced, and the identity of two other wanted men established. Ultimately these men were traced and arrested at Romford where they were hiding.

At the scene of the attack officers later found a woollen stocking loaded with $3\frac{1}{2}$ lb. of wet sand which the gang had used to attack Sergean Deans. Such were his injuries that he was seven weeks in hospital and on sick leave.

First recognition of his gallantry came in May when he was awarded £15 by the magistrate at Bow Street, but in September 1947 he was awarded the King's Police Medal.

Later that year, in December, his colleagues on the Flying Squad presented him with a silver cigarette case as a tribute to his courage. This is a rare tribute in the police force but the "Heavy Mob," as the Flying Squad is known in the criminal world, realized probably far better than anyone else the kind of courage needed for the task for which this tough young Scotsman readily volunteered.

They knew that it was due almost entirely to his fantastic courage, extreme coolness and self-control that this bunch of dangerous crooks were arrested and sentenced to terms of penal servitude varying from three to seven years.

It would be expected that a man of such calibre would eventually get promotion, and he did. In August 1955, he was awarded the rank of Detective-Inspector, and became the "Guv'nor" at Stoke Newington. But he stayed only a few years more, and in September 1959, he retired from the Metropolitan Police after 27 years service, and became security officer for a telephone manufacturing company.

CHAPTER FOUR

WOMEN DECOYS

WHENEVER there is a job of such known dangers as those which faced Sergeant Deans, Scotland Yard not unnaturally selects a man, or men, they know to be physically, and mentally, equipped for it. There are occasions, however, when the presence of a man, even in plain clothes, would completely nullify any attempt to catch the criminal.

This is particularly so in cases of indecent attacks on women. Perpetrators of this crime invariably choose quiet, isolated spots, or unfrequented lanes, and strike only when there is no one about but the victim.

He does not attack if there is a man in sight. He waits for the lonely woman, jumps on her in the darkness when he is satisfied no one else is about, and has his escape route ready should there be any unexpected interference.

Special watch on the area is generally pretty useless. The attacker is on the look-out for this and simply does not attack. How then can he be caught?

The police at Croydon were faced with this quandary when a dangerous, violent man haunted the mile-and-a-half-long Fairfield footpath, not far from East Croydon railway station, in November 1954.

His attacks on women walking home alone along that dark, wooded footpath were particularly serious inasmuch as they were becoming increasingly violent. His assaults were at irregular intervals and by an ever changing pattern. Uniformed, and even plain clothes patrols along the footpath were useless. The man was not seen; there were no attacks.

In the New Year 1955, the attacks became so vicious that the police feared that murder would be committed unless the man was caught. They realized, too, that there was little hope of catching him unless a trap was set—with a woman brave enough to act as decoy.

These experienced officers did not disguise the fact that any woman who was brave enough to walk along that footpath alone, and at night, would almost certainly sooner or later be brutally attacked; yet they found volunteers.

Several women officers at Croydon police station readily agreed to act as human bait and sometimes in pairs, sometimes alone, they walked along the pathway, ready and waiting for the dreaded blow.

Chief among these were Police-Sergeant Ethel Violet Bush, 39, and her colleague, Police-Constable Kathleen Flora Parrott, 39, and the story of their heroism ranks high in the history of the Yard.

On 20 February 1955, the attacker struck again. A 25-year-old married woman was walking home alone along the footpath when the man jumped at her from behind some bushes. She screamed and he dealt her a violent blow across the face. He was forcing her to her knees when a man happened by good chance to appear, and the attacker fled. All the hysterical woman saw of her assailant was that he was masked.

Sergeant Bush and P.C. Parrott started routine patrolling along the lane, often in plain clothes. Both fully realized the danger; both felt pretty certain that one night they would be attacked.

And on the night of 7 March it happened. P.C. Parrott, a married woman with a son aged 10, finished her duties at about 10.30 p.m., changed into plain clothes, and decided to walk through the footpath which was a direct route to her home. No other officer was about, but she had been trained in self-defence, and felt quite capable of dealing with the marauder if he appeared.

Kathleen Parrott walked straight up the footpath, and had almost reached the junction of Chichester Road when suddenly she heard running footsteps behind her, and before she could turn, felt an arm flung round her neck from behind. When she twisted her head she saw it was a man. The pressure of the arm increased and she began to lose consciousness.

She struggled fiercely, but the man dragged her to her knees. The officer knew then that if she did not get free in a moment she would be unconscious; so, in a last desperate effort, she hit at him over her shoulder with the torch she was carrying. She knew she had hit him, but she did not know where, and she heard the man say, "I won't hurt you if you stop screaming."

The plucky woman officer still struggled, but the man was too strong for her, and with his arm still gripping her neck he put his hand up her clothes from the back and under her skirt. She fought back, and eventually broke free from the stranglehold, and for the first time was able to turn and face her assailant.

Woman-Officer Parrott then saw that the lower part of his face was covered, and, despite the terror of the attack her reaction as a police-officer was instantaneous. She snatched at the mask so that she could get a look at the man, and, if possible, recognize him if she saw him again.

She saw that he was a man of about 28 to 30 years of age, about 5 ft. 10 in. in height, with brown hair—and the man himself was so startled by her action that she broke completely free from him, and bolted away.

She was later examined by a police doctor at Croydon police station and found to have injuries to her left knee, right thigh and face. In addition, there was severe bruising on both sides of her neck, which, according to the doctor, was consistent with very considerable pressure having been applied around it. In fact, such was the nature of her injuries, that she was on the sick list for five weeks, and had to spend most of that time in bed.

The assault on W.P.C. Parrott was the most serious since the series had started in November 1954, and the police had no information which would assist in the identity of the night-attacker other than that provided by the officer which, because of the darkness, was naturally sketchy.

However, the Yard men took such a serious view of these attacks, that from the very next day arrangements were made to keep the footpath under observation from dusk until midnight every night.

Detective-Sergeant Charman was put in charge of this observation, and he arranged for men detectives to keep watch from various vantage points along the path, but he knew that male officers were not sufficient to bring about the capture of this dangerous, lone miscreant.

He wanted women officers, women officers who would be courageous enough to patrol that footpath alone, and in plain clothes. And he found plenty of volunteers. No fewer than twenty volunteered to walk that frightening mile-and-a-half footpath, alone, and in darkness.

On the night of 8 March they started, somewhat comforted by the fact that male officers were stationed nearby, but fully realizing that they would most certainly be hurt before they could expect any aid. But apparently the attacker had been frightened by the courage of Kathleen Parrott, for several weeks went by and no further incidents involving the masked beast were reported.

Then, at 7.30 p.m. on the Saturday night of 23 April, the constant police vigilance was rewarded. Woman Police-Sergeant Ethel Bush, and Woman Police-Constable Treanor, were on the course of a normal patrol along the footpath in uniform when they saw a man lurking suspiciously among the bushes. As they passed him they saw him trying to hide still further.

His furtive actions were, shortly afterwards, noted by Police-Officer Kathleen Parrott who, despite her previous alarming attack, had once again volunteered for plain clothes duty along this dark, and dangerous, footpath. She told P.C.s Hillier and Sparks of her suspicions and, by an agreed plan, walked alone, prepared once again to be attacked.

And once again she was followed, but this time P.C. Sparks walked about thirty yards ahead of her, and P.C. Hillier followed the man who was following her. It was a tricky task to keep the man in sight as the footpath was twisty, and on one occasion when P.C. Hillier lost sight of the suspect, he hurried only to see him hide again in bushes by the side of the path.

There was no doubt now that this man was a prime suspect —but suspicion is not enough to convict, and later the officers saw him walk past them and disappear. A few minutes later these three officers met Sergeant Bush and P.C. Treanor and together they conferred and agreed a plan as to how this dangerous, but careful, attacker might be trapped.

W.P.S. Bush and W.P.C. Treanor returned to Croydon police station to report, and to suggest that they should change into plain clothes to lure the man into some action while other officers took up pre-arranged positions in hiding.

Shortly after 9 p.m., Sergeant Bush, dark-haired, and only 5 ft. 4 in. tall, left Croydon police station in plain clothes to act as the main decoy, and almost as soon as she started walking along the footpath a man was seen to leave a nearby recreation ground, and commence to follow her.

In the interval between her first sighting the man and changing into plain clothes six male officers had taken up strategic positions along the path, hiding behind walls and fences. W.P.C. Parrott was there, too, and the man passed within a yard of her hiding place behind a fence. She recognized him by the light of a street lamp as the man who had attacked her on 7 March.

Everything was set, the trap was laid, and Sergeant Bush continued on the most terrifying patrol of her life. She had seen, from the corner of her eye, the outline of the man start to follow her from the shadows of the recreation ground, and she knew that with the other officers well out of sight, he would attack her. As she approached a point from where P.C. Hillier was keeping watch the man was still following her, and P.C. Hillier had to bend down behind the wall where he was hiding to prevent himself being seen.

Then as soon as they passed he stood up and looked. He saw W.P.S. Bush still walking along at the same steady pace, looking neither to the right nor left, and he saw the man slowly catching up with her.

Then, when he was only a couple of paces behind her, he stooped and picked up a large "Y"-shaped piece of yew tree, and with both hands grasping this weapon he brought it with full force down on to the head of the defenceless woman officer.

This blow was partially softened by the felt hat Sergeant Bush was wearing, but it was severe, and watching officers were staggered that despite its severity she turned and grasped her assailant by the lapel of his jacket, trying to hold on to him until one of the men officers could reach her. But at that moment the man felled her to the ground with a vicious blow from his fist.

Hefty, 6 ft. Police-Sergeant Leslie Morgan with Alsation police dog "Skip" was the nearest officer in hiding, but he too had been forced to bend down behind the wall to avoid being seen by the attacker, and it was only on the sound of the blow —which he thought was a gun shot—that he again looked over the wall.

He saw the woman sergeant struggling with the man, and he saw him fell her to the ground with his fist, and he immediately sprang into action with most unfortunate results. The wall behind which he had been hiding had broken glass set in cement on the top, and as he was in the act of throwing his dog over, he accidentally, in the darkness, placed his hand on one of the pieces of glass and received a laceration from a finger to the wrist. (It later required ten stitches.)

Despite this severe injury he leapt over the wall, but he was so handicapped, that he landed on top of his dog, Skip, and injured the animal. And in the meantime the attacking man fled.

Woman Police-Sergeant Bush was taken to Croydon General Hospital and was found to have a "Y"-shaped laceration at the back of her head which required eleven stitches. Sergeant Morgan wrapped a handkerchief around his badly cut hand, and led a hunt of 20 officers for the masked marauder—but he had got clean away.

Later that night there was a conference of detectives at Croydon police station and officers who had seen the attacker, particularly W.P.C. Parrott, were able to give such a good description of him, that strong suspicion fell on one man—a man already known to the police.

Detectives went to the home of this 29-year-old labourer, and he was taken to Croydon police station where he strenuously denied the attacks even after being picked out by six witnesses at an identification parade. When he was charged, however, he admitted all the assaults along the footpath since November 1954.

He appeared at Croydon Magistrates Court and when he was committed for trial the chairman, Mr. B. Still, said, "The court would like to pay a tribute to the courage and devotion to duty of the women police-officers, especially W.P.S. Bush and W.P.C. Parrott. They voluntarily exposed themselves to the risk of serious injury which was in fact sustained by W.P.S. Bush. Their conduct was in the very best tradition of the Police and their courage was of a very high order. We would like to commend them and hope that their senior officers will take note of this commendation."

In due course the labourer appeared on trial at the Old Bailey and was sentenced to ten years imprisonment by Sir Anthony Hawke, the Common Serjeant, who said to him, "Your counsel has said everything that could possibly be said. If there is any question of your state of mind then the fullest investigation could be made by order of this Court with a view to seeing whether some kind of treatment could properly be effected within the power of the court.

"But the Doctor of the highest responsibility and knowledge has already examined you for that, and looking into your state of mind he is of the opinion that your mind is clear and healthy, albeit, possibly immature. You apparently suffer from perfectly horrible impulses which you knowingly gave way to with your eyes open. It is clear from the evidence that they are becoming progressively more dangerous. What emerges from this appalling series of events is that no woman is safe while you are at large."

Counsel for the defence had told the court that the defendant had said to him, "I want to stop this before I go and do something worse—before I go and commit a murder." Apart from these offences he was a perfectly ordinary chap, and he had a perfectly good work record.

What might have happened had not this man been arrested is unpredictable. What is certain is that it was entirely due to the gallantry of these women officers, gallantry described to me by a senior detective officer as being "almost beyond belief," that this most serious series of assaults was brought to an end. At the conclusion of the trial Sir Anthony Hawke called Sergeant Bush and P.C. Parrott to the well of the court and commended them on behalf of the court, and the public generally, for their "most conspicuous gallantry."

"I cannot imagine higher courage than you showed along that footpath with full knowledge, with your eyes open, that you might be, as Sergeant Bush was, the victim of a horrible and violent assault. The conduct of the police is always a matter of which we in this country can be proud. I think this country is entitled to be proud of you two officers. I think you have done a very great and gallant thing."

His added comment that he hoped "due notice would be taken in proper quarters" was followed on 14 June 1955, when both officers were awarded the George Medal—the first women police-officers in Britain to be so honoured.

They were presented by the Queen who said, "I am very proud of you both."

The citation said they "displayed outstanding gallantry, determination, and devotion to duty in bringing about the arrest of a dangerous criminal," and, "they acted as decoys in full knowledge that they might be the victims of a horrible and violent assault without any regard for their personal safety, and in keeping with the highest traditions of the Metropolitan Police."

Sergeant Bush had joined the force in 1946, and was promoted to sergeant in 1953, while P.C. Parrott joined in 1951. Sir Lawrence Dunne, then Chief Metropolitan Magistrate, presented them each with cheques for £15 from the Reward Fund at Bow Street, and said of their action, "If anyone can imagine a finer story in the history of the Metropolitan Police, I shall be pleased to hear it."

Few people in fact appreciate the important part played by women police in the maintenance of law and order, and in the prevention and detection of crime. They have the same regulations of service and discipline as the man, and exactly the same status and power. After two years service they become eligible for the C.I.D., and it is in plain clothes that they have proved of immense value.

Experience has shown that the presence of an attractive, well-dressed woman distracts attention from the male detective, and women detectives are often employed in this way, particularly when there is an awkward watching brief to be kept up on suspected criminals. Most crooks boast that they can "smell a C.I.D. man a mile off," but the presence of a woman often defeats them.

It so happens that a woman detective once played an important part in "guarding" me during the course of a murder inquiry. Three years after the murder of Miss Daisy Edith Wallis, who was stabbed to death in her Holborn Secretarial Agency office in August 1949, I recalled the hunt for her killer in an article in the *Evening News,* with remarkable results.

An anonymous letter was sent to me at the office. It said that the writer knew the identity of the murderer, and that he would lead me to him. He wanted a reward, but only if his identification was *proved* to be correct. And he suggested a public house in Holborn as a meeting place the following Tuesday. I was to insert an advertisement in the personal advertising columns of the *Evening News* if I agreed to meet him, and if so, I was to carry a trilby hat conspicuously in my left hand, to assist in identification.

This letter was seen by Chief-Superintendent Harold Hawkyard and Chief-Inspector (later Chief-Superintendent) Robert Stone, the Yard men who were in charge of the Wallis murder inquiry. Both agreed that it should be followed up. It had a ring of genuineness about it inasmuch as the writer wanted cash *only* if the man he pointed out was proved to be the killer.

The advertisement was duly inserted in the *Evening News* and the Yard men made their plans. I was to keep the appointment, and Superintendent Stone would keep an eye on me. If the man led me from the public house he would follow, and from then on we would "play it by ear"—just act as we thought best.

That Tuesday night I walked into the public house bar, and spotted in a quiet corner seat Superintendent Stone and a most attractive female companion. She was, of course, a woman C.I.D. officer, but no couple could have appeared more disarming or less conspicuous. Naturally no signal passed between us and I stood at the bar with hat in hand as instructed.

A few minutes after the appointed time of 6 p.m., a man entered. And immediately his actions indicated he was the anonymous letter writer. His hand shook violently as he stood near me and ordered "Half-a-bitter." Then he looked at me and looked at my hat. I half-smiled but he made no approach.

After a moment or two he shakily ordered another beer. I stood tense with excitement, and thought, Now, this is it. So evidently did the Yard man, because at that moment the woman C.I.D. officer went to the bar, stood next to him, and ordered a packet of cigarettes. I saw her take a surreptitious look at him before she went back to her seat.

Then, just as we thought things were about to happen the shaky man swallowed his beer in one great gulp, darted for the door, and disappeared into the street. Immediately the woman C.I.D. officer leapt to her feet and followed him. She was out of the door and into the street within a minute. But in that brief moment he had disappeared! Whether or not he suspected me (I am over 6 ft. tall) of being a police-officer or not we shall never know. Apparently he hid in one of the many blocks of offices nearby. We waited another half an hour but he never reappeared.

It was, however, a clever move on the part of the Yard men to have a woman officer at that rendezvous because even if the shaky man suspected me, I am quite certain he had no idea that the well-dressed man and woman quietly chatting in the corner seat were a couple of detectives.

Women officers, as already indicated, play a most vital part. Recently police-officers at Harlesden learned that three bandits were planning to rob the manager of a store on his way to his home in Wembley. They had to keep watch on these men without being seen, and their best "eye" was a woman detective. She disarmed all suspicion by the simple expedient of pushing a pram!

In fact the great example of cool heroism such as that displayed by Sergeant Bush and W.P.C. Parrott at Croydon did have a precedent; an act of similar courage which resulted in the award of the first ever King's Police Medal for Gallantry to a woman—a woman C.I.D. Sergeant in 1947.

None of the many women C.I.D. officers I have met looks even remotely connected with the Metropolitan Police Force, and Miss Alberta Mary Law was no exception. She had a mass of dark hair, sparkling eyes, and a great vivacity. Before the war she served behind a counter in Lancashire, but the job did not suit her; she longed for excitement. The war gave her her chance and at the age of 32 she joined the Metropolitan Police Force. By 1947 she had done so well that she was a detective-sergeant.

At about that time a number of women had been attacked on Tooting Bec Common, and officers there were faced with the same difficulties as those related at Croydon. The attacks were so persistent that desperate remedies were called for. Any woman walking across the common was not safe. She was knocked about and her handbag stolen.

Sergeant Law knew all this when she volunteered to walk alone, with handbag as bait, through the common at night; and on the very first night that she undertook this terrifying lone patrol, a man suddenly sprang at her, flung her to the ground, and hit her on the head with a bottle he carried as a weapon, before watching detectives could get at and overpower him.

The then Recorder sentenced the man to five years penal

servitude at the Old Bailey and said, 'His arrest was only possible by the extreme bravery and heroism of this officer. No one can speak too highly of her or commend her too strongly."

She was the first woman officer ever to receive the £15 from the Bow Street Reward Fund since it was established fifty years earlier, and in September 1947, the King awarded her the King's Police Medal for Gallantry.

CHAPTER FIVE

DOMESTIC SQUABBLE

To men of courage one of the most fascinating aspects of a policeman's job is its exciting uncertainty. This applies just as much to the uniformed police-constable on the beat as it does to the detective whose entire time is spent investigating, and dealing with the activities of criminals. They never know when the most normal routine inquiry will turn, without the slightest warning, into the most dangerous episode of their lives.

I have toured most shady areas of London with uniformed officers and detectives at dead of night, and have never failed to appreciate the skill with which these men deal with any, and every, eventuality. Yet no one realizes more than these skilled keepers of law and order just how easily the simplest incident can lead to extreme violence; how, without warning, the gun, the knife, and the cosh can be produced—and used.

Yet, with steadfast loyalty, they go about their jobs fighting, as best they can with their limited numbers, an ever increasing number of criminals, and a growing variety of crooked talent.

Every local station in the Metropolitan Police district has a defined area for which the officers in the station are responsible, and this area is known and referred to by them as "our manor." Every incident involving an officer on the manor is recorded, and I doubt if there is any police station in the whole of the Metropolis where there is not a record of some minor incident which, on investigation, has developed into a major crime.

Domestic squabbles on the "manor" are quite frequent, and often reported by the aggrieved husband or wife who, in the heat of the moment, demand police action. Drink, of course, more often than not plays its part in these quarrels, but the sight of a man in blue has a most sobering effect, and in hundreds of cases, in fact in most cases, a few words of kindly advice by the police is followed by a happy reconciliation, and no further police action.

In some instances, however, these domestic battles take on a more serious aspect particularly when a weapon is used, and one or more of the contesting parties is injured. In such an instance the offender may be charged with causing grievous bodily harm, and he, or she, may be detained until formalities are completed and a charge is made.

This is routine, and it was, therefore, regarded as little more than routine when there was domestic trouble in a home in the East End of London on the night of 2 June 1961, during the course of which a man's wife, his mother-in-law, and younger sister-in-law all complained of having received injury. Apparently the man lost his temper with them and struck out with a chair, injuring all three.

The complaint was duly recorded by uniformed officers who went to the house, and was marked for further investigation by the C.I.D. It looked on the face of it a straightforward charge of causing grievous bodily harm. No one expected this comparatively minor charge to explode into the murder of two senior uniformed officers, and the wounding of another, and one of the most dramatic gun and murder hunts in the East End of London.

On the day after the attack on the three women at roughly 12.45 p.m., the telephone rang in the C.I.D. office at West Ham police station. Detective-Inspector George Jones answered the call and learned within a moment that the caller was the man who had wielded the chair and injured his wife, and her mother and sister. "I understand you want to see me about the affair last night," said the man. "Can I come and see you? Can I speak to the officer who is dealing with it?"

Detective-Inspector Jones, who knew all about the previous night's attack, invited the man to call, and within a few minutes was confronted by a 6 ft. 1 in. tall, blond salesman, who identified himself as the wielder of the chair. It was evident that the man had telephoned from a nearby telephone box, and it was evident too that he realized he had badly hurt his wife and in-laws, and was contrite.

They talked for a while and there was nothing in the sales-man's attitude or behaviour which gave rise to any suspicion. In fact he behaved exactly as one would expect from a husband who had lost his temper and was now extremly sorry about it. Inspector Jones told him that it was in his favour that he had called at the station of his own accord, but he hoped he realized that each of the women was quite seriously hurt.

Once again the salesman expressed his extreme sorrow. "I went on my knees to them and asked forgiveness," he said, "but they started pushing me about so I lost my temper and hit them with a chair."

This, of course, was tantamount to a confession, but the inspector said nothing at that stage. He asked the tall salesman to accompany him into the C.I.D. office where he knew Detec-tive-Sergeant Lewis was on duty. They entered the office together, and the salesman stood beside the inspector while the sergeant, who was also aware of the fracas the evening before, took down the man's description of what exactly had happened during the family row at home the night before.

The man openly and readily admitted his guilt. Everything was quiet; nothing abnormal. Then, when this formal part of the proceedings had been completed, Detective-Inspector Jones turned to him and said that he would, of necessity, be detained while further inquiries were made. And, as is customary when police take such action, the officer ordered the man—now officially his prisoner—to empty his pockets.

The man started to do so with the eyes of the detectives on him. Certainly the officers expected nothing more than the usual garbage a man carries. But the first articles he produced and placed carefully on the desk at which Detective-Sergeant Lewis was sitting were six loaded bullets!

Both officers raised their eyes from the table in surprise, and at that same moment, without a second's hesitation, before even the officers could recover from their shock, he dived his hand into his right hand trouser pocket and pulled a gun which he pointed unwaveringly, and with considerable menace, at them.

The inspector made an involuntary, almost imperceptible, move towards the gunman, who was now backing slowly towards the door, but he was stopped as the German automatic was turned on him. "Don't be silly," said the officer, but the gunman ignored the warning. "You are not keeping me here," he replied, and with that he dashed through the C.I.D. door and down the stairs towards the main entrance to the station. Both C.I.D. men shouted an immediate warning.

At that moment, it was somewhere in the region of 1 p.m., P.C. Charles Edward Cox and P.C. Leslie Charles England were chatting to another officer at the foot of the stairs leading from the C.I.D. office, and they heard the detective shout, "Stop that man." They looked up, and saw the gunman run into the charge room, and across to the main entrance where he turned and pointed his pistol at them. He backed out of the station, and they saw him cross West Ham Lane and bolt into the West Ham Recreation Grounds.

In an instant the quiet formality of the police station changed into one of intensive activity. Here was a man with a gun, unquestionably loaded, running amok in the East End. P.C. Cox started chasing him and saw him run across the park, climb a fence, and disappear into Whalebone Lane.

Although on one occasion the blond salesman turned and pointed the pistol at him he did not fire, and P.C. Cox continued chasing after him across the park. Then the officer ran alongside the fence before climbing over in the hope that he would head the man off. But, by the time he vaulted over into Whalebone Lane there was no sign of him.

Meanwhile P.C. England ran to the back of West Ham police station, collected his motor cycle, and drove into the park where a number of officers had arrived. He learned that the gunman had last been seen in Whalebone Lane and immediately headed there where he joined up with P.C. Cox. Both questioned passersby as to whether they had seen a man running, and eventually found a small boy who pointed in the direction of Faringford Road, and said, "He went that way—and he had a gun!"

Back at the station an officer alerted Scotland Yard's Information Room of the escape and soon, while the searchers fanned out from West Ham police station, all radio patrol cars were ordered to join in the hunt.

P.C. England drove in the direction indicated by the boy, followed on foot by P.C. Cox who had now been joined by Police-Sergeant Frederick George Hutchins who was in plain clothes. Together they ran into Tennyson Road, a quiet Victorian road alongside a recreation ground where children were playing on the swings, slides and roundabouts.

It was Saturday lunch-time, and many mothers who went to their front doors to call their children for the midday meal were startled as they saw the man, still holding the gun, run past them, followed by the police. Several saw him turn into Faringford Road and shouted this advice to the pursuing officers.

Then, as the officers turned into this road, they saw him. Sergeant Hutchins said, "That's him," and with no thought of danger from the gun both men shot forward with the sergeant in the lead. Sergeant Hutchins sprang on the man's back and flung his arms around him trying to grab the gun. But the 6 ft. blond salesman was powerfully built, and in an instant he swung violently around, flung the sergeant off his back, and ran forward for about five yards. The sergeant went to tackle him again, and was within a foot of him when the man turned, raised his pistol, and deliberately shot him.

P.C. Cox was only a few feet away, and saw it all happen, but he did not hesitate. He lunged forward to grab the gunman, but at that same moment the gunman turned the pistol in his direction and fired again. P.C. Cox fell to the ground, and Sergeant Hutchins, who had been staggering with the impact of the bullet, collapsed across his legs.

Several men and women in Faringford Road that afternoon witnessed this cold-blooded, deliberate shooting. Most were so shocked that they were momentarily rooted to the ground as they saw the tall, blond man turn again, and with the pistol held menacingly at elbow level, flee further along the road. P.C. England, on the motor-cycle had just turned into the road in time to see his brother officers shot down and he at once rode up to them.

Sergeant Hutchins, who had been shot in the abdomen, saw him ride up, but his only thought was that this man must be captured. He lifted his head and ordered P.C. England, "Get him, Les. Get him, he's got us." P.C. England shouted to the bystanders to call an ambulance for the wounded men, and then made off again in pursuit of the gunman who had turned off into Tennyson Road which runs into Romford Road.

At that moment P.C. England was the only officer on the direct trail of the man, a man he now knew would not hesitate to shoot to resist arrest. He knew the danger; he knew he was taking his life in his hands; but this former Irish Guardsman drove on with grim determination, his only thought being the capture of the maniacal gunman.

He soon caught up with him, and saw immediately that he still held his gun at the ready. As he got to within twenty feet of the man he suddenly turned his motor-cycle on to the pavement and drove straight at him. He got to within about three feet, still cool, calm and determined, when the gunman turned, and again raising his pistol, fired a shot at him. P.C. England, with great presence of mind, braked sharply, swerved, ducked his head down on the tank of his machine, and the shot missed.

As soon as he had fired the shot the gunman turned and fled again, weaving in and out among the aghast bystanders. For a few moments there was chaos. Mothers shouted to their children to take cover. Others went into their homes to get blankets and pillows to help and comfort the wounded officers.

One boy who had seen the shooting ran into a café and yelled, "A gunman has just shot two coppers," but in his excitement and near-hysteria the people there sitting quietly having their meals thought it was a youthful leg-pull, and for some moments no one believed him. Another youth who had wit-

c

nessed the shooting could not believe that it was real life. He went up to the gunman who had momentarily stopped to reload, and with all innocence asked, "Is that a real gun, mister?" "Yes, son," replied the man, before he once more dashed off.

By this time he was approaching the end of Tennyson Road, and just at that moment Inspector Philip Pawsey, aged 40, driving a police wireless car on a lone patrol, turned into it. The time was 1.20 p.m., and there is no proof, but there can be no doubt that he had heard the radio messages sent out from the Information Room at Scotland Yard about the escaped gunman, and had driven there in the hope of assisting in the capture.

As soon as he entered the road he saw the man, still carrying the pistol in his hand, come running towards him. He drove his car across the road and jolted to a halt. P.C. England saw what was happening, realized the immense danger, and signalled the inspector to keep away.

Inspector Pawsey ignored the warning and as the man got to within a few feet of the car, he opened the door as if to get out. The man immediately pointed the gun at him, and the Inspector pulled the door to. And the gunman did not then fire. Immediately he had passed the car, however, the Inspector again opened the door and started to get out. The gunman turned on the instant and shot him at point blank range. Eyewitnesses said later it was from a distance of three to four feet.

The Inspector collapsed in the driving seat and the gunman bolted again. P.C. England was on the scene in seconds, and as he drove past the car he heard the dying Inspector call out, "Get after him." He saw the Inspector reaching across the car trying to get hold of the radio microphone which linked him with Scotland Yard—his very last thoughts being to give warning of the danger and the whereabouts of the man with the gun.

P.C. England, 34 years old, with less than eight years service in the force, had now seen two of his superior officers and a colleague deliberately shot down, but he stuck grimly to the trail. Hereabouts, however, he was badly hampered by traffic;

by cars and vans and lorries which had just driven into Tennyson Road, and the drivers of which had no idea of the desperate chase that was in progress.

The officer weaved his lightweight motor-cycle in and around these vehicles, and eventually reached Deanery Road just in time to see the gunman turn right at the far end. He accelerated down this road and, at the bottom saw a large furniture van parked by the south pavement with the gunman standing and half-hiding behind it. He tried to approach, but each time he did so the tall, blond salesman pointed the gun at him. P.C. England had no doubt that he would be shot if he got closer, so he wisely kept his distance, but still keeping the man in sight.

Eventually help arrived in the way of a civilian cyclist who P.C. England asked to go to a police box in Romford Road and inform the police station of the gunman's whereabouts: to tell them he needed help. So dangerous was the situation now that there is no doubt that if the gunman stayed where he was then officers at the station would arm themselves and endeavour to bring about an arrest at gun-point.

He was in fact now a murderer—though this was not then known to P.C. England who watched him, ready for any action, from a distance of a few yards. Eventually the gunman realized that the officer had sent for assistance, for, after a few minutes rest, he made off across some waste ground in Deanery Road, and entered the rear of a house facing on to Romford Road. So the P.C. drove around there quickly, and approached another officer who was standing nearby. This officer told him that the man had got into a yellow lorry which they could then both see passing traffic lights heading east towards Forest Gate.

Determined not to let the gunman out of sight the officer chased after the lorry, ordering his colleague to ring the Yard with this latest information. Then help arrived in a most unexpected form. As he drove along P.C. England was joined by a man on a motor-scooter to whom he shouted across these instructions: Overtake that yellow lorry, get ahead of it, and go to Ilford police station and tell them the gunman is on it.

Ask them to set up a road block, stop and search it. But be careful, he is armed and will shoot.

This quick-thinking plan worked. P.C. England kept the lorry in sight until it reached Ilford police station where it was stopped and searched. Two men were on it—but neither was the gunman. A sadly disappointed P.C., had been badly misinformed!

Back again went the search to the house in Romford Road where the gunman had last been seen. Scores of officers joined in. House and shopkeepers were questioned and passersby stopped. But there was no sign of him. By this time every police station and police car in the whole of London had been alerted in a great hunt for the *killer*. It had now been learned that Inspector Pawsey had been shot in the heart and had died almost immediately. Sergeant Hutchins had died shortly after his admission to Queen Mary's Hospital, but he was revived for a time by cardiac massage. A doctor opened his chest and massaged the heart which began beating again after about three minutes. He was given artificial respiration and a blood transfusion, but he died at 4.30 p.m.

News of these senseless, meaningless murders of two officers on duty sparked a wave of justifiable anger throughout the force. Both officers were well known and respected by their colleagues, and another senior officer had to break the sad news of Inspector Pawsey's death to his wife Muriel, who had had his lunch ready at 1 p.m. at their home in Ilford that day, and who had not been unduly worried when he did not arrive on time. She thought he was on "another job" and was accustomed to irregular timekeeping. Inspector Pawsey was 40 years old and had been in the force 15 years.

Imagine, too, the tragedy the news brought to the Wanstead home of Sergeant Hutchins who was 49, and had served 28 years in the force. His wife and two children, a son of 22 and a daughter of 14, were already planning happy surprises for his 50th birthday in eight days time.

P.C. Cox was lucky. The bullet aimed at him hit a thick seam in the jacket he was wearing, and his life was saved. It damaged his stomach and affected the nerves in his left leg, but after some time in hospital he was able to resume light duties.

That same evening when the news of these brutal, senseless murders became known the whole of London was shocked. No one could understand why this inquiry on a minor charge should suddenly have erupted into a double murder. Orders were issued from the Yard to every police station, "This man must be captured at all costs."

Every officer who went on patrol that evening was given the name of the gunman and his full, detailed description. Known haunts of the gunman were kept under constant observation. Friends and relatives were warned that they must telephone the police immediately they caught sight of him.

But there was no clue to his whereabouts and no sign of him until 8.30 p.m. that same evening. What happened to him in the meantime, where he had been hiding, no one knows but at 8.30 p.m. he revealed his whereabouts in a most dramatic way. Mr. Nelson Sullivan, a journalist, and a man of considerable experience as a crime reporter, was on duty that night for a Sunday newspaper, taking calls from members of the public who thought they might have some news to give.

It was exactly at 8.30 p.m. that his phone rang, and when he lifted the receiver he heard a man's voice say, "I am the killer. I am the man who killed the policeman." And the man went on to give his name, and told the story of the murders in such detail that within minutes Sullivan was convinced that this was no hoax, and that he was indeed in conversation with the murderer.

The journalist signalled to a colleague sitting nearby, and indicated to him that he should listen-in on a link telephone on the desk. He continued to talk to the man who told him that at that moment he had a gun pointing at his own chest and was going to pull the trigger.

Sullivan told the man not to be silly. He kept on talking to him and questioning him. Eventually he persuaded the man to give him the number of the telephone box from which he was ringing—Wanstead 4199. His listening colleague immediately telephoned this information to Scotland Yard, who within a few minutes, located the telephone box and ordered patrol cars to the area to surround it.

Mr. Sullivan had played his part particularly well, and soon police-officers were cautiously approaching the box where they could see the man still talking—the call, in fact, lasted fourteen minutes. Evidently, however, he had seen the officers. There was a muffled report, and the man was seen to throw his arms in the air, and fall backwards against the door. He was taken to Whipps Cross Hospital where he lay critically ill for a week until he died the following Saturday.

The officers were buried that same day, and no warmer tribute has ever been paid by the East End than that paid to these men who were killed in the course of their duty to them, and to the force. More than 200 wreaths were handed in at the local station with such words as, "To a Good Copper"—"From the Stallholders of Stratford Broadway." More than 2,500 police, including representatives of every force in Britain, lined the route.

No fitter words could have been found by the Rev. Lawrence Pickles, vicar of St. Peter's, Barkingside, who said at the service, "People don't join the police force with any sense of heroics, but just go in to do their duty. If it involves them in danger, as it often does, then they still carry out their duty to the best of their ability."

At the inquest at West Ham Coroner's Court on 21 June, the Coroner, Mr. J. Milner Helme, recorded a verdict that the gunman had murdered Inspector Pawsey and Sergeant Hutchins, and that he killed himself, but before he did this he said he wanted to express his commendation of the police concerned in the case. And he added:

"The country has come to expect a high standard from the police, and in this case the police knew they were dealing with an armed man. They were all taking their lives in their hands in the course of duty and each of them did that duty without hesitation. I think the whole handling of the case on the evidence we have had shows great courage and devotion to duty on the part of the police. They all knew they were likely to be shot and we owe them a debt of gratitude."

What of the widows of the officers? An immense feeling for them swept the country and gifts ranging from pennies to pounds, and eventually totalling more than £5,000 poured into West Ham police station. Questions as to their welfare were asked in the House of Commons with this result:

Mr. David Renton, the Under Secretary at the Home Office said, "The police pensions regulations provide for the payment of special pensions to the dependents of regular police-officers who die as the result of injuries received in the execution of their duty. Mrs. Pawsey's total benefit, including police pension and industrial injuries payments, has been provisionally assessed at £10 1s. 1d. a week, and Mrs. Hutchins at £10 7s. 0d. a week."

P.C.s Cox and England were each rewarded with £20 from the Metropolitan Magistrates Court Reward Fund, and later it was announced that both Inspector Pawsey and Sergeant Hutchins had been awarded the Queen's Police Medal for Gallantry—at this time a posthumus award.

P.C. Charles Cox was awarded the George Medal, and P.C. England the British Empire Medal.

CHAPTER SIX

TWINS SEE THE QUEEN

SOME encounters between the police and armed villains have had happier endings. They have brought joy and thankfulness to a family. Pride in the achievements of a husband and father has overshadowed the proximity of tragedy. No one except those in the force, or those who work closely with it, can appreciate the almost constant anxiety of a police-officer's wife and family.

Policemen, like journalists, talk an awful lot of shop among themselves, but they are not inclined to discuss their jobs with people on the outside, unless perhaps it is with their families. Wives, particularly, appreciate the hazards. They have seen their men return to their homes shot, or coshed, or knifed, but they have rarely flagged in their loyalty and support. They know that tonight, and every night, their husbands can never let up in the constant, never ending war with the criminal.

So it was with P.C. Henry William Stevens and his family, and their story of heroism which had a happy ending. It came to fruition on the morning of 25 November 1958. That morning the officer awakened his wife and their 7-year-old attractive twins, Lorraine and Paul at their home in Seward Road, Bromley, Kent, and they started preparing for a day they will remember probably above all others in their lives.

P.C. Stevens, aged 30, with five years experience in the force, donned his smartest uniform and his wife prepared her newest frock. Lorraine had her fair, long pigtails tied with red ribbon bows which perfectly matched her cherry red hat. Paul gave his black shoes an extra polish, and his blue coat was spotless.

Never was there a prouder moment for the Stevens family, for on that memorable day P.C. Stevens had been commanded by the Queen to attend Buckingham Palace to receive from her hands the George Cross for his exceptional heroism. And strict rules laid down for investitures at the Palace had been broken to enable the twins to attend and watch the ceremony with their mother.

It is decreed that only two guests are permitted at such functions, but the Stevens could not possibly take one twin without the other. They explained their problem to the Lord Chamberlain's Office. They felt sure, they said, that if the Queen knew of their predicament she would agree with their request, and both twins could attend.

Back came the reply which gave P.C. Stevens so much joy: "We have considered your case, and I have very much pleasure in telling you that you will be allowed to take three guests."

It is reasonable to assume that on his way to the Palace that day P.C. Stevens gave some thought to the slim, dark-haired young man whose nefarious activities had triggered off the battle which resulted in this journey. Here, on the one hand, was the officer with his family trained in mutual love, trust, obedience and respect. There, on the other side of the picture, was the slim young man at that moment in gaol. A criminal. A man with no respect for law and order. No trust. No obedience. A wicked man, a man who started crime with a cosh, and proceeded by stages to the knife and the gun.

It was the clash between these two great forces which led to their meeting on the night of Saturday, 29 March 1958, when P.C. Stevens had taken his first step to appointment as a detective by becoming an *aide* to C.I.D., and he was on duty in plain clothes in a police car at Bromley, Kent, with two other police-officers.

At about 7.55 p.m. they heard a police radio message directing another police car to a house at the junction of Bickley Park Road and St. George's Road at Bickley, where a burglar alarm system had given an alarm. This device had been installed in his home by the owner, Mr. Frederick Pickles, a manufacturer, because it had been burgled several times previously. Such alarms are connected directly with Scotland Yard, or the nearest police station, and give instant warning of an intruder unaware of its existence.

As the car carrying P.C. Stevens and his colleagues was in the neighbourhood of the house they decided that they too would investigate. Officers on wireless patrol duty are always keen for action, and they reached the house within a few minutes—before the car which had received the direct order had arrived.

Detective-Constable Moody and the driver, P.C. Wanstall, entered the front garden to search round the sides of the house, while P.C. Stevens went alone to the rear, passing a high garden fence which ran along St. George's Road.

He hurried quietly along and nothing happened for the first thirty yards or so. Then, suddenly, about five yards ahead he saw a man appear on the top of the wooden fence from the garden of the house, and jump into St. George's Road. There was a gas street lamp about five or six yards on the other side of the man and the detective had a good view of him. He saw that the man was about his own build—6 ft. and slim—and that he wore a grey coat and dark trilby hat.

As he dropped from the fence he saw the officer who shouted to him, "I am a police-officer. Stop." The man took no notice and bolted to the other side of St. George's Road and then away in the direction of a railway bridge. As he got to within about twenty yards of the railway bridge, where there was another street lamp, the man, who was only three yards or so in front of the officer, partly turned as he ran.

And P.C. Stevens saw that he was pointing a shiny metal gun at him. He held it in his right hand and shouted, "Stop, or you'll get this." The officer ignored the threat, and continued running towards the man and got to within reaching distance of him when there was a flash from the gun and he heard a report. At the same moment he felt a severe blow in his mouth, and his face went dead.

Despite the shock, the pain, and the blood, and despite the fact that he now knew he had to deal with a desperate armed man who would not hesitate to shoot again, P.C. Stevens threw himself on the man, grabbed the gun with his right hand, and wrenched it from him.

P.C. Stevens had an electric battery torch in his left hand and he caught the man round the neck with his left arm pushing him against the iron railings at the side of the railway bridge. They fought desperately and with all their strength, and at this time the officer was the stronger of the two. After a minute or so the gunman relaxed, stopped struggling and said, "All right, I'll give in. I've had enough."

His back was towards the officer at this time and he was being forced against the railings. Then, as the officer eased his grip, the man suddenly grabbed him in a most sensitive part of the body, causing the officer intense pain and forcing him to further release his hold. Whereupon the gunman again broke away, and ran back along St. George's Road towards Bickley Park Road.

P.C. Stevens shouted for help. He was bleeding extensively from the mouth, and he could feel broken pieces of teeth in his mouth, but he still ran after the man who, after about forty yards, turned round and tried to run round him along St. George's Road. He failed, and once more the plucky officer grabbed him, and this time struck out with the torch he was carrying.

The housebreaker still struggled violently, and P.C. Stevens, weakening with every moment, realized he could not hold him much longer. Once again the gunman slipped from his grip, but the officer summoned all his strength into one mighty effort and succeeded in grabbing him by his jacket and coat at the back of his neck. He was dragged along the road, but he held grimly on. Then, suddenly, the bandit wriggled his shoulders and arms, and slipped out of both jacket and coat.

P.C. Stevens, still with the jacket and coat in his hands, felt faint and weak, and fell to the ground. But even then he was not beaten. He got to his feet again and saw his man disappearing over the railway bridge. He ran after him, but by the time he reached the bridge the gunman had disappeared.

At that moment his colleagues came running up and he handed the gun, jacket and coat to Detective-Constable Moody. He saw this officer pick up a black trilby hat which had fallen from the man's head when he first chased him.

When the three officers had arrived at the house they split up as is usual in such cases—to try to cover every retreat open to a suspect. When P.C. Stevens went around to the rear P.C. Wanstall went to the left of the house and Detective-Constable Moody to the right.

P.C. Wanstall forced his way through a privet hedge and wire mesh fence in the grounds and reached the back garden when he heard P.C. Stevens call for help. He jumped the wooden fence and saw his colleague struggling with a man about seventy yards away along St. George's Road. As he ran towards them he saw the man wriggle free from his jacket and coat and bolt towards the railway bridge.

As he ran past P.C. Stevens he saw that his colleague was bleeding and that he was holding his face in his hands. He heard him shout, "I have been shot." P.C. Wanstall ran after the man over the railway bridge but he had disappeared in the darkness. He ran back to P.C. Stevens and found him leaning against a garden fence still holding the vital clues he had wrested from the gunman.

Detective-Constable Alfred William Moody, who had gone to the right side of the house, found a leaded window leading to the lounge had been broken and he started to enter the house by this window when he heard his colleague call for help. He, too, climbed the fence into St. George's Road but he was behind P.C. Wanstall.

Ordering P.C. Wanstall to take P.C. Stevens to hospital he searched nearby woods, and organized an immediate intensive search of the area for the gunman. But there was no trace of him.

P.C. Stevens was taken to Bromley Hospital and operated on. It was found that if ever a man's life was saved, literally by the skin of his teeth, then that officer's was that night. The

.22 bullet, fired at point blank range, had smashed three or four lower teeth, shattered part of his jawbone, and lodged in his tongue. Only the boney barrier of his jaw and his teeth had prevented the bullet entering his brain!

All the resources of Scotland Yard went into immediate action to identify and capture this desperate gunman. And they had, thanks to the great courage of P.C. Stevens four vital clues —the jacket, the coat, the hat and the pistol. They found that the .22 pistol was an unusual plated type rarely seen in this country, and this, together with the hat, coat and jacket, was taken to the Yard Forensic Department for microscopic and fingerprint examination.

On the jacket of the suit which the gunman had discarded detectives found a makers name tab. This line of inquiry was followed and within a matter of hours Detective-Inspector (later Superintendent) H. Bland, who was in charge of inquiries, had learned that it had been sold not long before at a shop in Deptford.

Detectives went to this shop, searched the files, and quickly learned that the jacket they now had in their possession had been sold to a man they knew. A man with a criminal record, and a man who was known to the underworld of crime as The Terror. Officers in South London knew him well, and they knew he fitted the description of the 6 ft. slim man who had shot P.C. Stevens.

The Terror was not born to be a criminal. He just preferred that way of life. As a youth he was rebellious and cruel, and soon took to thieving. It was as a teenager that he first tangled with the law when he was caught for housebreaking, theft, and assault on the police. On that occasion he attacked a police-constable with a lead-loaded piece of rubber hose and was sent to Borstal.

Borstal treatment did not improve him, and three years later he was caught again and sentenced to twenty-one months imprisonment for warehouse breaking. He had not been released very long before he stabbed a man with a carving knife and received four years imprisonment.

It looked on the face of it that there was little doubt that it was The Terror who had shot P.C. Stevens. But he had not been known to have used a gun before. At any rate Detective-Inspector Bland and his men were most anxious to talk to him and Scotland Yard issued this description of the man they wanted to see: "Age 27, 6 ft. 1 in. tall, sallow complexion, dark curly hair, dark bushy eyebrows, slim build, pointed chin, and long thin face."

He was not named to the Press, but every police-officer in the Metropolis knew him, and detectives in South London knew his haunts and his associates. They noted that with the description of him the Yard Chiefs had added the words, "This man is dangerous."

When a dangerous gunman like this is on the loose no effort is spared to get him under lock and key before he can do any further damage. But The Terror knew that within a very short while the Yard would be on his trail, that they would, through his discarded clothing, have traced the shooting to him, so he went to ground.

Detectives kept constant watch on his home, addresses he was known to frequent in South-East London, and his criminal associates. Members of the Flying Squad hunted the under-world of crime for the slightest whisper that would lead them to his hiding place. Eventually word came to the searching officers that The Terror had secured another gun and six bullets, and that he had been heard to boast that five of these bullets were for any policemen who tried to arrest him, and the sixth was for himself.

Then on 9 April through their secret channels, channels that will never be revealed, the Flying Squad men received the tip they had been awaiting. They learned that The Terror was hiding in an hotel in Queensborough Terrace, Bayswater. They planned their raid in the early hours of 10 April when they hoped he would be in bed and asleep.

And the man chosen to lead the raid was Detective-Sergeant Peter Vibart (later Detective-Superintendent); a man without fear, and an officer with considerable skill and unsurpassed knowledge of the underworld. He organized his raid on the hotel at 12.30 a.m., and took with him Detective John Perkins and a number of other officers to cover every possible exit.

Quietly, but efficiently, the hotel was surrounded while Vibart and other officers spoke to the management, secured a master key, and tiptoed up the stairs to the third floor bedroom which The Terror had booked under the name of R. L. Johnson—which is certainly not the name with which he was born. Stealthily the officers fitted the master key and turned it—but the door would not budge. The gunman had fixed it from the inside ready for such an emergency.

Vibart signalled to his colleagues, and they stood clear of the door while the burly, hard-as-nails sergeant, stood back and then lunged forward with his full weight. The door smashed in, and as it fell back Vibart and his men went in over it and sprang on to the bed which was at the far corner of the room.

A startled Terror made a grab for the gun under his pillow —but a fist landed on his jaw, and he realized that further resistance was useless. When the officers took the gun he said, "If that had been loaded you would have got it as well." It was, in fact, unloaded.

Detective-Sergeant Vibart searched The Terror's room, and in addition to the pistol under the pillow he found a small canvas holster, and a hatchet concealed by underwear. In a raincoat behind the door he found a knife, and a carboard carton containing pepper. When asked about these discoveries the gunman said, "They are for my protection, and to settle debts in my own way."

At 1.30 a.m. that day The Terror was seen at Bromley police station by Detective-Inspector Bland, the officer in charge of the inquiries into the shooting of P.C. Stevens, who said to him, "I have reason to believe you shot at P.C. Stevens at Bickley at 8 p.m. on 29 March. You will eventually be charged with the attempted murder of that officer."

The Terror replied, "I know it's down to me. I bought the gun, and the one you found tonight, from a man for £1. He had eight. I have had it. You carry on. You have got my jacket. If

I come the old story it was nicked from me, it still boils down to the same thing. You can do what you like."

What he meant by this, of course, was that he realized that the Yard had traced him from his jacket, and that he knew it was hopeless for him to expect the police to believe the story told by so many criminals that the article which led to his identification—in this case the jacket—had been stolen from him earlier and that it was the thief—not he—who had done the shooting.

Later in the day at Court The Terror was asked if he had any questions for the inspector who repeated what had been said at the police station. "I have nothing to say," he said. "There is not a word of truth in it."

On 24 April when he appeared at Bromley magistrates court again The Terror was faced by P.C. Stevens who produced the chromium plated .22 pistol with which he had been shot. It was then revealed for the first time that because of a defect the gun needed rather an effort to fire a second shot. When it was found it contained one spent and five live rounds. One of the five bullets had a mark on it which suggested that the hammer had struck against it, but it had not fired.

After P.C. Stevens had given evidence and shown his wound, the Chairman of the Bench said to him, "You acted with great braveness and great determination, and I have not the slightest doubt your colleagues are aware of this and that the Commissioner's attention has been drawn to it. But the Bench wish to say your fellow citizens must be relieved and proud to think that men like you and your colleagues are on duty at night as in the day time to protect them."

On this occasion five further charges were preferred against The Terror. Two accused him of wounding William Mills and Frank Dunn in London with intent to cause grievous bodily harm. Another alleged that he broke into a store at the Artillery Museum, The Rotunda, Woolwich, and stole six fire-arms valued at £81, the property of the Queen, and the others that he broke into the house at Bickley and stole a table lighter and a pair of scissors.

In May The Terror appeared for his trial at the Old Bailey and strenuously denied that he had shot at the officer with intent to murder him. He said that he intended to hit him with the pistol which he always carried with him ready to fire. "It is part of me," he told the jury, "I always carry a loaded gun."

After deliberating for four hours the jury failed to agree on the intent to murder charge and the Judge discharged them from giving a verdict. The following day Mr. Christmas Humphreys, for the Crown, said in view of the disagreement he did not propose to put the defendant on his trial again on that count. Another jury was sworn in and the man was formally found not guilty of attempted murder.

The Judge then addressed The Terror in these words: "In my view you are a wicked and dangerous man, and I feel it my duty to send you away for a long time. If you had been convicted of shooting with intent to murder the sentence I am about to pass would have been even longer.

"This was a vicious affair involving a police-officer. You are a lucky man that Providence intervened to save you from a charge of capital murder. If I am any judge of such matters it might well have resulted in your conviction and that might well have been the end of you. You seem to have no respect for persons, law or property."

He then sentenced The Terror to ten years imprisonment for shooting at P.C. Stevens with intent to cause him grievous bodily harm, four years for wounding the two men Mills and Dunn, twelve months for the breaking and entering at Bickley, and twelve months for receiving a stolen hat and overcoat— all the sentences to run concurrently.

As soon as he heard the sentence The Terror said, "I will bet money I never finish it," and then just before he was taken to the cells he added, "I would like to congratulate the police on maintaining a high standard of collusion and perjury."

Mr. Justice Ashworth then called P.C. Stevens before the Court and said to him, "Stevens, I would like to say this to you, and I am quite sure that the Jury, though they have not agreed on their verdict on count one, will completely endorse what I have to say, and I am sure Counsel for the defence will too: in my view your conduct was of the very greatest gallantry, and really is a performance of which you might be rightly proud and I hope your senior officers will take account of it."

In July, Sir Laurence Dunne, then the Chief Metropolitan magistrate at Bow Street awarded £15 cheques to P.C. Stevens, Detective-Superintendent Vibart (he had been promoted in the interval) and Detective Constable John Perkins who was with Vibart when they broke into The Terror's room at the Bayswater hotel, and referred to the story as the finest to emerge from the annals of the London Police Force "for a considerable time."

On 21 October 1958, came the announcement that P.C. Stevens had been awarded the George Cross and the story of his problem—would the twins count as one for entry into the Palace. One feels that none of the scores who received honours from the Queen that day in November would not have approved of the rule-breaking which allowed P.C. Stevens to take his twins with him. Only sheer grit and courage enabled him to carry on with such determination after he had been shot, and to secure sufficient evidence for the arrest and conviction of The Terror.

No wonder when the twins left the Palace that day they said, "We felt so proud when the Queen smiled at Daddy and gave him the medal."

CHAPTER SEVEN

FACTORY RAID

No police-officer ever knows when he will come face-to-face with a gun; a gun held by a desperate criminal who will not hesitate to use it to avoid capture. Such men are, almost invariably, men like The Terror, men with prison records, men beyond correction or reform. Men, for example, like Scarface.

Young, strong, 5 ft. 6 in. tall, fresh-complexioned and hazel-eyed, he had an ugly scar on the left temple which gave him this nickname in the underworld of crime. His record was such that he knew his capture on any further crime would result in a very long period of detention behind bars; so he carried a gun for "protection." He also carried it to terrify the victim of any proposed hold-up. He was known to Scotland Yard as one of the most dangerous criminals in the country.

He carried a gun during the war and, like a number of young men who lived by crime and scorned any honest job, decided to do so when the war was over. In June 1945, during the invasion of Germany, he deserted from his regiment and ran riot, with the result that on his capture and eventual court martial he was sentenced to fifteen years penal servitude for four cases of rape, and other charges of assault and robbery.

Eight years of this sentence were remitted, but it was not long before Scarface escaped from military custody, stowed away in a ship, returned to this country apparently undetected, and resumed his life of crime in the Metropolis.

One day he thrust a pistol into a garage owner's stomach, but police-officers were nearby to prevent the proposed robbery, and they caught him. After a struggle, during which he again produced his gun, the officers were walking along a viaduct parapet to take him into custody, when he suddenly leapt over, dropped thirty feet, and got away.

He laid low but five months later was traced to a house in Clacton-on-Sea. When officers burst into his bedroom he leapt through the window and dropped sixteen feet to the ground— into a waiting officer's arms. He had been trapped, and in March 1946, at Essex Quarter Sessions, when aged 21, he was sentenced to fourteen years penal servitude for attempting to steal a car, having a loaded pistol with intent to endanger life, and with having a pistol at the time of committing an offence, and at the time of arrest.

He was lodged in Wakefield Gaol, and for about six years he gave all the indications of being a model prisoner. He was put in the category of a "Trusty," and employed as a night stoker. In December 1952, he used this position as a Trusty to fashion himself a grapnel hook which he attached to lengths of electric light cable. He threw the hook over the wall of the prison, climbed the cable and escaped.

Every police force in the country was alerted to keep a lookout for this most vicious criminal. Members of the public were warned in the Press and by radio, "If you see this man do not tackle him. He is dangerous. Send for the police." Watch was kept on his home and on his associates, but the police completely lost track of him. It was evident, too, that criminals who knew his hideout were too friendly—or too frightened—to squeal.

In actual fact he was back in London, hiding out with a gang of thugs in the East End, and heading six men who bullied, plundered and robbed. Four of them held up the guests at a private party in a public house in January 1953. One of them, and there is little doubt it was Scarface, carried a gun, and the rest were armed with coshes. They stole all the money, watches and rings carried by the men, and all the cash and jewellery from the women.

Scotland Yard heard underworld whispers that Scarface was the leader of this gang, each member of which wore a red scarf to use, when necessary, as a mask. Every clue was followed and hundreds of reports inquired into. He was No. 1 on the wanted list. It was not until early in February 1953, that under-cover men gave patient detectives a clue that led to his capture after a fight which resulted in the award of two George Medals to officers he could not keep at bay, even with his loaded gun.

On Monday, 2 February, Detective-Inspector Edward Bowler of Hackney police station received a tip that a gang was planning to steal the wages bag of a clothing firm in Chatham Place, Hackney, on the following Friday. It was the custom at this factory of Messrs. Cedra Mantles Ltd., to collect the wages for the factory staff every Friday from their branch in Bethnal Green.

Mr. Leslie Moutrie, one of the employees, had for the past two years left the factory at about 4 p.m., collected the wages totalling between £700 and £800, and returned with them in a brief case by taxi about 5 p.m.

Inspector Bowler told Mr. Benjamin Izen, manager of the factory, about the proposed hold up, and suggested that he should make arrangements to vary the normal procedure and get the money collected by a different person at a different time. On the following Thursday, the 5th, he saw the factory manager again, and was told that Mr. Izen had planned for the money to be collected earlier the following day, but he would send Mr. Moutrie on the trip as usual, and at the same time—but with an empty brief case.

The detective-inspector noted the plans, said he would be watching the factory the next day, and suggested also that Mr. Izen should keep watch from his office window about the time the wages normally arrived, and report to Hackney police station if he saw any suspicious persons loitering nearby.

On the Friday at about 4.15 p.m., with Detective-Constable Thomas Halley, the inspector commenced his observation on the factory. He drove slowly towards Chatham Place, and saw two suspicious-looking characters lounging against the windows of a newsagents shop. They were talking, and he saw one point in the direction of Cedra Mantles Ltd. The officer drove past and around the block to have another look at these men, and this time saw that they had been joined by a third. All three were standing in the gateway of the nearby Morningside School.

Inspector Bowler and his detective parked their car nearby and kept surreptitious watch on the men. They saw two of them leave the school, walk slowly along the pavement to the factory, look all around, at the factory, and up and down the street, and then re-enter the school gateway out of sight.

One or the other did this on several occasions and the inspector ordered Detective Halley to telephone for assistance. It looked obvious that these three men were planning to rob. Halley did so, and in case any of the men spotted him, he borrowed three large empty cardboard boxes from the premises from where he made the call, and walked down Chatham Place with them. No one would suspect a detective carrying such boxes!

In the meantime Mr. Izen had been keeping watch from his window as instructed and at 4.20 p.m. saw three men standing at the end of Ram Place, just below him. He watched them for a while, didn't like the look of them, and rang the police station as Inspector Bowler had suggested.

At about 5.5 p.m. or 5.10 p.m. Mr. Leslie Moutrie, as previously arranged, phoned him from a nearby post office to ask if it was all right for him to come in. Mr. Izen told him it was, and then kept watch for the arrival of the taxi.

A few moments later he saw the taxi arrive, and then suddenly a man came up the stairs towards him—he was one of the three he had seen loitering outside. Mr. Izen yelled at him and the man turned menacingly and put his right hand inside his left breast jacket pocket. The factory manager lunged at him with a piece of iron he picked up, and the man bolted into the street closely followed by some of Mr. Izen's employees. He shouted to them to leave matters to the police whom he knew were about.

Meanwhile Scotland Yard's Information Room had been alerted, and at 5.5 p.m their warning message was received by

a "Q" car, a disguised police radio car, which had been stand-
ing-by in nearby Wick Road. In this car were Detective-Constable Edward Snitch, aged 35, a married man with a 4-year-old
son, P.C. George Baldwin, aged 28, married, and P.C. George
Dorsett, aged 28, married with four children, the driver.

They made off straight away through Morning Lane, left into
Retreat Place, right into Chatham Place and then went towards
Morning Lane where they saw a crowd of people running towards them. P.C. Dorsett stopped the car outside a factory and
heard the chasing men shout, "There's two of them." And the
officers saw two men turn the corner from Chatham Place into
Meeting Fields Path.

P.C. Dorsett immediately backed the car into the entrance of
the factory, turned round, and went after the men. They followed them through Rivag Place, across a bombed site at the
end, and towards the junction of Mead Place and Cresset Road
where the two men separated. The Yard car was then about
ten yards behind them, and P.C. Dorsett pulled up.

P.C. Baldwin jumped out and ran after the man who ran to
the left. Detective Snitch ran after the man who kept to the
right, and followed him into the grounds of Melbourne House,
and then along the left hand side of the building where he got
to within about five yards of him.

At the corner of Collent House the officer called out, "Stop,
I am a police-officer." The man half turned round and shouted,
"Keep away from me you bastard, or I'll put a bullet through
you." He then saw the man reach under his raincoat with his
right hand, pull out a revolver, and point it at him. He was
then about three yards away.

Detective Snitch did not hesitate. He went on after the man
and a shot was fired. The officer stumbled and fell to his knees
and then saw that P.C. Dorsett had joined in the chase. He got
to his feet and again went after the gunman. P.C. Dorsett had
seen Snitch fall as if shot, but he, too, carried on. Both closed
with the man who then fired two more shots!

P.C. Dorsett got hold of the man's head and Detective Snitch
grabbed his gun hand and after a short struggle, wrested the

gun from him, and the two officers quickly overpowered him.
Detective Snitch unloaded the revolver, a Smith and Wesson .38,
and put three spent cartridges and three live rounds in his
pocket.

In the meantime P.C. Baldwin caught up with his man in the
garden of Lennox Buildings and, after a short struggle, overpowered and detained him.

P.C. Snitch was later examined by a doctor and found to be
suffering from a superficial wound about one inch long on the
outer side of the right eye. There was also a hole in the belt
of his raincoat which was obviously made by one of the bullets
fired later. It appeared that he, like P.C. Stevens, had escaped
death by inches. And the man who had fired the gun was no
other than Scarface.

At first he denied his identity, but he was known to Detective-
Inspector Bowler who had seen the shooting, and who later
identified and arrested the third man in the proposed hold-up.
When he was searched at Hackney police station that night a
further 12 rounds of .38 ammunition was found on Scarface
as well as a black patent leather holster on a white strap.
When he was cautioned and told he would be detained he
replied to the officer: "—— you, you've caught me. I'll take
the lot."

Detective-Chief-Superintendent Stephen Glander, who has
since retired from the force and is now Security Officer for the
Midland Bank, later took charge of inquiries, and he learned
that Scarface had been hiding out in a flat in Sydenham, Kent.
He searched the flat and found a second pistol and a further
100 bullets hidden in a folding bed there.

In March all three men appeared at their trial at the Old
Bailey and all were found guilty and Mr. Justice Streatfeild
said that, "It says much for the gallantry of these two officers
(Snitch and Dorsett) that they arrested such a man as this."

When Detective-Chief-Superintendent Glander read the previous records of the men it was pointed out that the one who
bolted with Scarface had not long before served eight years
penal servitude for the manslaughter of Captain Binney, R.N.,

who was killed when trying to stop a car in which the man was trying to escape from a jewel shop robbery.

But whether this man, or the third man in the attempted hold-up, knew that Scarface carried a gun will never be known. Curiously enough Scarface was most insistent that the man who ran with him did not know, "At no time did I tell him I had a gun or a cosh," he told the police, "and he is quite innocent of any weapons at all. I shall get the book and I don't want anyone else to suffer for me."

On 20 March Mr. Justice Streatfeild sentenced Scarface to gaol for life, "For the first time in my life, and, I hope, the last," adding, "You are a thoroughly dangerous man. You are a danger to society every moment you are at liberty."

Scarface smiled imperturbably, bowed, and said. "My lord, you are too generous." The second man received five years imprisonment, and the third man three years.

Once again the unfaltering courage of the police had brought about the capture of one of the most dangerous criminals in the country. It has never been revealed whether Snitch and Dorsett recognized Scarface. I don't think it matters if they did. Here was a menace to society and their only thought was that he must be overpowered. Personal thoughts of their own safety never entered their minds.

After passing sentence Mr. Justice Streatfeild said, "Before parting from this case I would just like to express the appreciation and admiration of the Court for the great gallantry and devotion to duty shown by Detective-Constable Snitch and P.C. Dorsett, and I very much welcome the rider which the Jury have added to their verdict expressing a similar appreciation. I trust that the conduct of these two police-officers which in my view deserves the highest commendation will be drawn to the attention of the Commissioner of Police."

Yet another tribute came when the three officers mostly concerned in the capture—Snitch, Dorsett and Baldwin, were summoned to Bow Street to receive cheques of £15 each for their heroism from the Bow Street Magistrates Reward Fund.

Sir Lawrence Dunne, then the chief magistrate, said, "It is regrettable that there should be desperate men in this country who do not hesitate to fire at unarmed police-officers. But," he added, "it is commendable to know that the Metropolitan Police Force still produces men so imbued with the spirit of the Force that they do their duty so well and serve the public in this way."

The final honour came on 28 October 1953, when Detective Edward Norman Snitch and P.C. George Edward Dorsett received George Medals from the Queen at Buckingham Palace. P.C. Baldwin went with them and received the Queen's Commendation for Brave Conduct for his courage and determination in the face of danger in making the second arrest.

The story of the courage and determination of P.C. Dorsett does not end with that honour. Fortunately, although no one disputes there are still far too many guns in the hands of criminals, it is rare indeed that the same officer has to face the menace of a gun more than once. Yet P.C. Dorsett did. And once again he behaved with such cool heroism that he was awarded a bar to his George Medal.

It happened on a Saturday afternoon just over five years later, in December 1958. He had been on night duty, and was asleep in bed at his home in Hampton Road, Chingford. Suddenly his slumbers ended, and he was awakened by an explosion which seemed to have come from just outside his window.

He sprang out of bed, ran to the window, and saw in the street below a youth of 16 pointing a double-barrelled gun at a neighbour's house. It was evident that the boy had fired the gun at a window, and he looked as if he planned more mischief.

P.C. Dorsett did not hesitate. He threw on a dressing-gown, ran into the street, and called to the boy to draw his attention. The boy turned towards the officer, the gun pointing in his direction. "Now, don't be silly," said P.C. Dorsett quietly. "Don't be silly." And as he spoke he walked slowly towards the youth.

The youth then raised the gun menacingly at the officer and

said, "Keep away. I am not frightened to use this." P.C. Dorsett repeated quietly, "Now, don't be silly," and he continued to walk quite quietly and slowly, pace by pace, until he got a yard or so from the muzzle of the gun.

Then suddenly he jumped. He knocked the gun aside, grabbed the youth, took away the gun from him and arrested him. Neighbours who had heard the previous gun shot stood aghast as they watched from their windows, and saw the officer on that terrifying walk.

On the way to the police station P.C. Dorsett found that the gun contained a 12-bore cartridge, but it was not cocked. When he pointed out this to the boy he replied, "I know it was not cocked because I pulled the trigger and nothing happened."

"So," said the officer, "you did intend to shoot me, did you?"

"Of course I did," replied the boy.

Inquiries were made, and it was learned later, and stated at the juvenile court, where the youth duly appeared, that the youth had threatened to kill the father of his girl-friend, aged 15, because the father objected to their association and had ordered them not to see each other again. The youth took his brother's shotgun, went to the house of the father and his girl-friend, and fired the gun at the window.

What further damage this boy might have done had not P.C. Dorsett been on the spot will never be known. There is little doubt that he was mentally disturbed by the order demanding the end to his love affair, and the citation noting the further award said there was little doubt that if the youth had fired P.C. Dorsett would have been seriously injured or killed.

In February 1959, Dorsett received a Commendation from the Commissioner, "For devotion to duty whilst off duty, and outstanding courage and determination in tackling and disarming a youth armed with a loaded shotgun." And in June of that year it was announced that he had been awarded a bar to his George Medal.

I believe that in these two awards P.C. Dorsett established a record for police bravery and that to date he is the only officer with a George Medal and Bar, and the only one to be so honoured in the first instance by the Queen, and in the second by the Duke of Edinburgh.

It is an ironic fact that this officer fell and broke his arm while engaged in the seemingly harmless task of painting his house in 1962 and had to be found other duties in the Force because of his disability at that time.

CHAPTER EIGHT

A WOMAN'S PHOTOGRAPH

RELATIONS, and co-operation between the Press and the Metropolitan Police, have always, in my years of experience, been of a very high order. Each has a healthy respect for the other, and there is a constant flow of information and advice. This is maintained through Scotland Yard's Press Bureau, the entrance to which is by way of one of the two green doors situated near the main entrance gates to Scotland Yard along the Victoria Embankment.

Here it is that crime reporters attached to newspapers and news agencies receive from a rota of Press Officers, drawn from the Civil Service, up-to-date information on current crime, and assistance on any moves about outstanding major crimes, such as murder. Officially Metropolitan police-officers are not permitted to impart news directly to a newspaper man—hence the Bureau whose officers give background advice, and do their best to answer questions from the Pressmen who are in direct touch with their newspapers from that office.

This close co-operation is of the utmost importance. It is through this Press Bureau that the Yard men issue descriptions of people they want to interview in connection with a crime. On occasion this has been eminently successful, and has had rapid results, but the difficulty with descriptions more often than not is that they could frequently fit so many people. Who, for example, could recognize a man wanted for interview in connection with a murder, from such details as these:

"Aged between 25 and 30, about 5 ft. 4 or 5 ft. 5 in. tall with very dark hair brushed back and worn long in sideboard style.

He is of square sturdy build of Italian appearance, and on the night of the murder was wearing a white open neck tennis shirt, brownish trousers, and was carrying a light coloured jacket."

Apparently no one, for this was the official Scotland Yard description of a man they were—and still are—most anxious to talk to in connection with the murder by stabbing of Miss Daisy Edith Wallis in the Secretarial Agency office she ran in High Holborn, in August 1949. It was issued within about forty-eight hours of her murder, and it is of a man seen running from that block of buildings on the evening she died.

Yet this man is still at large. No one has ever come forward with the slightest evidence that might lead to his identification. Descriptions are too often insufficient to lead detectives to the person they think could help them in the solution of a crime.

Now and again, however, there have been cases where Scotland Yard have been in possession of a photograph of a wanted suspect, but have been unable to issue it to the Press because its publication could interfere with the course of justice. It could, possibly, lead to some doubt on the question of identification by a witness in court. Pictures of wanted persons are published usually only when the question of identification is of no importance, and when their is sufficient evidence of another nature to warrant an arrest.

This is the story of a crime where publication of the photograph of a woman led to the capture of a murderer within a few hours; and the conviction of a man who had shot and killed a police-officer on duty. Yet this man had walked the streets of London for three days undetected before the photograph of the woman appeared in most, if not all, the national newspapers.

Events which led to the dramatic capture of this gunman, started on the evening of Friday, 13 February 1948, when P.C. Nathaniel Edgar, aged 33, kissed his wife and two small sons. aged 5 and 3, good-bye, and set off for a special patrol in the Wades Hill area of Winchmore Hill in North London. There had been a spate of burglaries in the district, and Edgar, an officer of promise, was proud of the fact that he had been specially selected to try and catch the person, or persons, responsible.

As an *aide* to the C.I.D. he was in plain clothes, and he was very keen because he was aware that any particular ability he showed on this assignment might earn him selection as a detective. He met, as arranged beforehand, P.C. McPartland who was to join him on the night patrol, and together, in the darkness, the two men set off on a tour of the district.

It was just another job to these young, keen officers. The sort of job that is carried out constantly without the public being aware of it. Scotland Yard cannot reveal its plans. To do so would alert the thief. Edgar and McPartland quickly patrolled the streets, keeping a constant look-out for anyone acting in the least suspiciously. Both had been well trained in the art of detection, and in keeping observation without drawing attention to themselves.

For an hour or so there was nothing unusual. They saw the men and women returning to their homes from their City jobs, and then round about 7 p.m. the tree-lined streets and avenues became quiet. A few minutes later they spotted a hatless young man acting with such suspicion that they decided to keep him under observation. He was looking intently at the houses he passed, looking in fact as if he was about to break into the first empty one he could find.

Keeping such a man in sight in a quiet suburban street without him seeing you, or arousing his suspicion that he is being followed, is extremely difficult. Yet, for the best part of an hour the two officers shadowed him successfully. But up to that time he had made no move to warrant his apprehension. Then, in the darkness, they lost him.

P.C.s Edgar and McPartland held a hurried conference, and decided that the best way they could get on to his trail again would be to separate. This they did, realizing of course that the man must still be within a matter of a hundred yards or so from them, and that one or other was bound to catch up with him quickly.

Fifteen minutes later the peace of Wade's Hill was shattered by three gun shots fired in quick succession. Several people living in nearby houses heard the shots. Several went to their front doors and looked out, but they saw and heard nothing further, and returned to the warmth of their fires, unaware that within some yards of them a police-officer lay dying.

At about the same time Mrs. Mary Laing and her brother were in Broadfield Avenue, Winchmore Hill, on their way to Wades Hill to visit friends. Suddenly they heard the shots which sounded, they said later, "Like three sharp whip-like cracks." Seconds later they saw a man tearing around the corner from Wades Hill at a tremendous pace.

It was as if all the furies were after him, said Mrs. Laing, and both she and her brother wondered what had happened. The running man soon disappeared into the night, and the couple turned into Wades Hill. They had walked a few yards when they heard groans. They searched, and within a few minutes found P.C. Edgar lying face downwards in the entrance to one of the houses.

They raised the alarm and within a few minutes Dr. E. S. Samuels, who lived in Wades Hill, and who had also heard the shots, was treating the dying officer, caring for him until the arrival of the ambulance which had been summoned.

Within minutes of the alarm being raised senior detectives from Scotland Yard were on the scene. The garden path in which the shot officer lay was cordoned off, and soon every resident nearby in Wades Hill was being questioned as to whether they had seen or heard anything suspicious that night. It was apparent at the outset that P.C. Edgar had most probably been shot by the man he was seeking—the housebreaker.

He died later that same day—Friday, 13 February! He had three bullet wounds. One in the right thigh, the fatal one, in the small of the back, and one in the upper part of the right leg. Each of the shots had been fired from close range, and the downward track of the bullets indicated that the officer was standing, probably talking to the gunman, when the trigger was pulled.

These facts strongly supported the original theory that the

(Top) Police hunt murderer in Onslow Square. *(Bottom)* Guenter Podola who shot and killed Det. Sergt. Purdy

Det. Sergt. E. J. Chambers   Det. Insp. W. Deans

W.P.C. Parrott and Sergt. Bush

Tennyson Road, Stratford, where Sergt. Hutchins
was killed by a gunman

Police surround telephone box in Wanstead where a killer was shot

Twins see the George Cross awarded to their father,
P.C. Henry Stevens

P.C. George Dorsett

Det. Con. Edward Snitch

P.C. George Sinclair

P.C. Leonard Bocking

Inspector Moody *(right)* sees again the man he overpowered in a Stockwell boarding house

A youth is charged with murder at Croydon

An arrest following a shooting in Cartwright Gardens

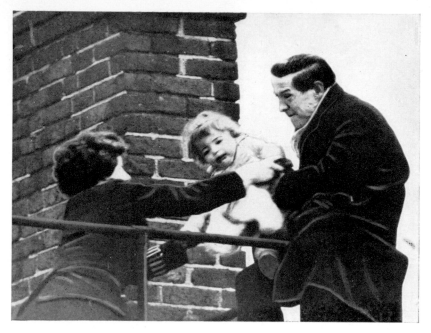

Thousands saw this dramatic rescue of a child in Bloomsbury

Sergt. J. A. Robson leads the way from another "Action Station"

murderer was the housebreaker, or at least someone the officer suspected of being the housebreaker. And the fact that this man would shoot to avoid the possibility of arrest indicated that he was a man with a record. And such a criminal record that he knew that another conviction would result in a long term of penal servitude.

P.C. McPartland was able to provide an important clue in the description of the man that he and P.C. Edgar had been shadowing, and there were so few people about at that time that there was little doubt that P.C. Edgar caught up with him, and was questioning him when he was shot down.

All the clothing and possessions of P.C. Edgar were examintd by detectives, but it was in the officer's official police note-book that a vital clue was found.

In that book, the last pencilled entry, which must have been written that evening, was the name, the identity card number, and an address of a man—a man known to the police as a deserter from the Army!

Of great significance, too, was that P.C. McPartland told his senior officers he had seen the notebook earlier in the day and was positive that the entry of the man's name was not in it then. Further, he was able to say with complete confidence, that he had been with P.C. Edgar until they separated a few minutes before 8 p.m., and during the time they were together no entry of any kind had been made in that book.

The picture was clear. P.C. Edgar must have made the entry between a few minutes to eight and 8.15 p.m., when he fell mortally wounded. And there could be no doubt that the man named in his book was his murderer.

These facts were not revealed at the time, but next day Scotland Yard issued through the Press Bureau the name of a man they witshed to see. A man, they said, who was aged about 25, 5 ft. 8 in. tall, fair haired. And the great hunt for him started.

No effort is spared in any murder; but when a fellow-officer is killed by a crook the Yard men forget time, forget days off, forget everything but the fact that this killer must be caught. And as soon as the description of the killer appeared in every newspaper hundreds of reports poured in that he had been seen in various parts of the country. Every single one was investigated with meticulous care, and every known haunt of the suspect visited and watched. The address that the man had given P.C. Edgar was that of his mother who said she had not seen him for some considerable time. Day and night watch was kept there in case he decided to return home.

Within forty-eight hours of this most intensive inquiry detectives learned, on particularly good authority, that a 27-year-old married woman was in all probability still in the company of this man. She had left her husband and family for him, and she had still not returned. On 17 February Scotland Yard issued a photograph of this woman, the mother of three children, and said they wanted information of her whereabouts as they had reason to believe she might be with the wanted man.

In fact they had received a statement from her husband that his wife had run off with this man with whom she had been known to be most friendly before she disappeared from her home in Camberwell. So, on the 17th the woman's picture appeared on a number of front pages with an appeal to landladies and apartment housekeepers to report to the nearest police station if they knew anything of her whereabouts.

Publication of this woman's photograph brought immediate and startling results from a boarding house run by Mr. and Mrs. Edward Smeed, in Mayflower Road, Stockwell. At 7.30 that morning Mrs. Smeed, as usual, went to the front door to fetch in two morning papers that had been left. As she casually opened one of them she glanced at the picture of the woman, and then stared harder for that woman she was convinced was at that moment in one of her bedrooms with a man.

She called her husband who was shaving. He looked at both papers, and had no doubt about it. This was the woman wanted for questioning by the police, and who at that moment was in bed with a man she had described as her husband. And this man could be, probably was, the gunman who had shot P.C. Edgar.

Mr. Smeed hurriedly dressed and ran from the house to

telephone the police. On his way to the telephone he met War Reserve Police-Constable George Searle, aged 53, showed him the picture in the newspapers, and told him that the woman and her "husband" were asleep in his front top bedroom.

P.C. Searle told Mr. Smeed to return to the house while he telephoned for assistance, and within a few minutes, whilst he kept observation on the house, he was joined by P.C.s Dennis Wheeler, aged 38, and Robert Hyde, aged 42, who were on duty in a patrol car nearby, and who were instructed by Scotland Yard's Information Room to go to Mayflower Road and join up with P.C. Searle.

Wheeler was in plain clothes, and he, to avoid arousing any suspicion, left the car some distance from the house, and walked there. After he had talked to Mr. and Mrs. Smeed he had no doubt that the killer was with the woman in the bedroom above him.

Every officer engaged on this murder inquiry knew that the man was still armed, and that, in all probability he would shoot again to resist arrest. It was essential that he should not escape, that some well-devised plan should be arranged to surprise, overwhelm him, and get him into custody. P.C. Wheeler wisely sought further help and advice. He remained in the house and sent P.C. Foster to Brixton police station and was shortly joined by Inspector William Moody, 41-year-old, 6 ft. tall, 16-stone ex-footballer.

It was shortly after 8.20 a.m. that the inspector entered the house, faced with the problem as to how best he and his colleagues could capture a man they knew to be in possession of a gun. He questioned the Smeeds closely as to what was the normal procedure with relation to the "married" couple upstairs.

Mrs. Constance Smeed explained that she advertised furnished rooms in local shops, and on Saturday, 24th January the man arrived, booked a room for himeslf and his "wife" at 30s. each for bed and breakfast, explaining that his wife would arrive later. On the Monday he returned with the woman, and they moved into the room.

It was, she said, her usual practice to take them their breakfast of tea and toast and marmalade at 8.30 a.m., knock on the door, tell them that breakfast was ready, and leave the tray outside the door.

"Do just that today," the inspector instructed Mrs. Smeed. "Behave normally and please do not be frightened. When you knock on the door, leave the tray just as you do normally, and walk back down the stairs at the same pace you usually do. Please do not hurry."

It was essential that the normal programme be followed, and that the gunman's suspicions should not be aroused. Mrs. Smeed prepared the tray, and with heart atremble, walked up the stairs followed closely on tiptoe and scarcely daring to breathe, by P.C. Wheeler, Inspector Moody, P.C. Hyde, and P.C. Searle, in that order. She placed the tray on the floor outside the bedroom, knocked on the door, and called, "Here's your breakfast." The man called back, "O.K.", and Mrs. Smeed walked back downstairs.

The space outside the bedroom door was very narrow, and there was only just sufficient room for P.C. Wheeler and the inspector to flatten themselves against the door. There was not enough room for P.C. Hyde on the landing, so he waited two or three steps down, and P.C. Searle even further down, but still in view of the bedroom door.

The inspector and Wheeler waited quietly, their eyes glued on the door, waiting for it to be opened. After a moment or two they heard the sound of the key of the door being turned quietly in the lock. Then the handle of the door turned slowly and gently, and the door was opened cautiously for about an inch.

They caught a brief glimpse of the man they wanted in vest and pants. He peeped through the crack of the door, saw the officers standing there and immediately slammed the door in their faces. He did not have time to lock it, though, and the two officers heaved themselves at it, burst into the room, and saw their man running towards the bed which was around and behind the door.

They saw the gunman leap across and on to the bed, and

dive his right hand under the pillows; but by the time he had done that the officers were on top of him. P.C. Wheeler, who was slightly in front, flung himself across the lower part of the man's body, and the inspector threw himself towards his head and arms.

As Inspector Moody did this he saw the man pull a gun from underneath the pillows, and turn it in his direction. But the officer was too quick for the gunman. At that same moment he pushed the man's arm up, and tore the gun from his hand.

Immediately on the heels of these two officers came P.C.s Hyde and Searle, and within a second the gunman was overpowered. Then came a voice from underneath the bedclothes, "What is going on? Let me get up." And there was the woman, the woman whose photograph had led to this dramatic arrest.

Inspector Moody told her to get out of bed and get dressed, and while still holding the man on the bed, said to him, "I have reason to believe you are the man wanted, and I am taking you to Brixton police station for inquiries." He then said, "Is this gun loaded?" The man replied with venom, "That gun's full up, and they were all for you, you bastards."

In the police car shortly after leaving the house the man said to the inspector, "You were lucky. I might as well be hung for a sheep as a lamb." When he was put in a cell detectives examined the gun and found nine rounds of ammunition in it, eight in the magazine, and one in the breach. The safety catch was in the "unsafe" position!

At his trial at the Old Bailey in April of that year the gunman pleaded that he had no intention to kill, but said he had shot P.C. Edgar in the leg to get away because, as a deserter from the Army, he knew he would get three years imprisonment if he was caught. And he related exactly what had happened. It proved an identical picture to that which the Yard detectives had built up from the evidence they had.

He said he was walking through Wades Hill when P.C. Edgar stopped him, and asked him for his identity card. The officer then made a note of his name, address, and identity card number. Evidently seeing that the man's address given was in South

London the officer asked him what he was doing in that area of North London.

The gunman said he told the officer he was there to visit a friend. P.C. Edgar, evidently highly suspicious, asked who the friend was and where did he live. The gunman, still trying to keep up his bluff, said he would take the officer to him. They walked a little way along Wades Hill until they came to a house the gunman indicated to be that of his friend.

Then, as they entered the gateway of a house the man had chosen at random, he saw a light in one of the rooms and realized he could carry his attempted bluff no further. P.C. Edgar's insistence had called it.

He carried his gun, a 9 mm. German Luger automatic in a belt strapped in front of him, and when he then produced it that night, he said, P.C. Edgar put his hand on it, pressed it down, and it went off.

On 20 April 1948, this 22-year-old gunman was found guilty of murder, and sentenced to death—but this was a sentence the Judge and the law knew would never be carried out. Only six days before his trial started the House of Commons had voted for a five years suspension of capital punishment. And Mr. Chuter Ede, then the Home Secretary, had announced that sentences on those condemned to death were to be commuted to penal servitude for life.

In pronouncing this sentence of death on this gunman a 400-year-old ritual at the Old Bailey was swept aside. Mr Justice Hilbury did not wear the black cap, and a new and shorter formula was used. He said to the prisoner: "The sentence of the court upon you is the sentence prescribed by law—namely that you shall suffer death by hanging." The "Amen," usually pronounced by a chaplain, was omitted.

And in the following month it was announced that the gunman had been granted a reprieve. Fourteen years later, in April 1962 he was freed. This is about the average term of imprisonment served by those sentenced "for life", providing, of course, that the prisoner behaves in prison and does not attempt to escape or break any of the many gaol rules.

On 26 July 1949, all four officers responsible, by their courage and daring, in out-manœuvring this murderer—Inspector Moody, and P.C.s Wheeler, Hyde and Searle—were awarded the King's Police Medal for Gallantry at Buckingham Palace.

No story could more amply illustrate the importance and the value of close co-operation between the Press and Scotland Yard. It became known during the inquiry that even on the day after the murder this gunman walked the streets of London with the woman, undetected and unsuspected, by the thousands of people he passed.

His capture typifies the necessity of team work in the battle against crime—the Police, the Press and the Public. Mr. and Mrs. Smeed acted with speed and discretion. It needed unusual courage for Mrs. Smeed to take that tray as she did to the killer's bedroom. She said later, "You can imagine how my heart was beating as I tried to walk normally and unhurriedly. And then as I waited at the foot of the stairs I was almost sick with anxiety."

CHAPTER NINE

READY FOR THE UNEXPECTED

INSPECTOR MOODY and his colleagues expected trouble that morning, and were prepared for it. Speed and surprise were essential on their part, for there is no doubt that they knew they would have to face a gun unless they overpowered the gunman before he had time to reach and draw. Public co-operation had given them time to plan. None of the officers concerned carried a gun, though I do not doubt Inspector Moody could have applied for one, and would, in the circumstances, have been issued with it.

On far too many occasions, however, police-officers meet trouble, serious trouble, when they least expect it. Often they face danger when they are alone and in plain clothes; and no one, except perhaps the criminal, realizes that the man desperately trying to prevent damage to life or property is a detective, or a constable, in plain clothes.

On occasions such as these the reaction of the public varies. Some officers recall with gratitude the unhesitating, and often gallant, assistance they have had from men and women who have seen them struggling against great odds. Others have bitter memories of the lack of public support when they have been outnumbered and beaten to the ground, with the resultant escape of vicious criminals.

P.C. Frederick Mark Stone, a man who has done a great deal for the public, must have mixed feelings about public aid to an officer in dire trouble. He was 53 years of age, and an Assistant Warrant Officer at Marlborough Street magistrates court when he met trouble at a most unlikely time and place

—at 11.45 a.m., on a fine April day in busy, bustling Sloane Street, Chelsea.

He was one of many officers who, before that April day in 1951, had already won recognition for his courage. After service in the Merchant Marine he joined the Metropolitan Police in April 1921, and his first beat was along the Thames Embankment—the nightly home of so many vagrants.

P.C. Stone got to know a good many of these down-and-out men and, in his way, tried to befriend and help them. Several who showed some promise knew the hospitality of his home where he took them for food, rest, and counsel. In 1928, when one of the vagrants threw himself into the Thames from Westminster Bridge, P.C. Stone dived in after him and saved him. Then he and his wife nursed the man back to health and got him a job. For his courage in that rescue he was awarded the King's Police Medal.

This officer was one of many who, when off-duty, enjoyed helping others. He helped in the running of sports clubs to keep youths off the streets, and was something of a boxer, wrestler, and Rugby footballer himself. When war came he spent many hours helping people whose homes had been damaged or destroyed by bombs. From a wide area round his home in Kennington people came to him for help and guidance.

Then in 1941 came further recognition of his bravery, and lack of personal regard for his own safety, when the lives of others were at stake. A building received a direct hit from a bomb, and several people were trapped in the cellar. P.C. Stone unhesitatingly entered the building which was in danger of total collapse, and helped all those trapped to safety. For his heroism in this venture he was awarded the British Empire Medal.

At 11.45 a.m., on 17 April 1951, he was in plain clothes, engaged in the seemingly harmless task of serving some processes in Sloane Street, when once again he was called upon to show his courage, this time in the face of a gang of three men who had planned a smash and grab robbery at the premises of Messrs. Dibden Ltd., the jewellers.

This gang had planned their raid with precision, having taken into account the fact that Sloane Street would be busy at that time of the morning, and that they might expect some interference from members of the public. One man was to drive the stolen car, the second was to smash the jewellers window with a metal bar he carried, and the third man was to guard him with another metal cosh with which he was expected to keep at bay anyone who dared to try and interfere with their plans.

They went that morning to the car park in the centre of the road between Cromwell Road and Thurloe Street, and stole a car, a saloon Vauxhall, which they thought would be suitable for their purpose. The fact that the owner had locked all the doors and taken away the ignition key presented no undue problem for these experienced villains.

Roughly at 11.45 a.m. the staff of Messrs. Dibden were alerted by a series of blows struck at their windows; then the shattering of glass; and when they ran into the street they saw a man reaching into the window trying to grab a handful of jewels.

Then one of the staff saw another man standing in the middle of the pavement with a weapon above his shoulder threatening anyone who approached him or the man in the act of robbing the window. At that moment they saw a short, dark man run with great speed across the pavement and hurl himself on the back of the man at the window.

That man was P.C. Stone, though no one at that moment was aware that he was a police-officer. He was walking on the west side of the street, going towards Knightsbridge, when he heard the crash of glass. He looked across and saw that one man had just broken the window of the jewellers; another was standing beside a nearby car, holding a rod or stick with a large knob at the end, dancing about in a threatening attitude towards several people who had stopped because of the crashing glass. The driver of the car was lying back in the seat.

But in that brief moment between hearing the window shatter, and the time that he started darting across the road P.C. Stone's training as a policeman saw and noted several facts. He noted that the man threatening bystanders was about 5 ft. 8 in. or 9 in. tall, of athletic appearance, swarthy featured, and dark haired. The driver wore a dark suit, or overcoat, and a dark, trilby hat; the third man, at the window, had his back to him, and his left hand in the window, when the officer pounced.

He, in his own words, "Kept an eye on the man in the car in case he had a gun," and then went straight at the man at the window. "I dived at his legs, but unfortunately he got the first one in with the steel bar he had used to break the window. Before I could disarm him he gave me more blows with the bar. I held on to him and got the bar away from him.

"Then the other man—the man who had been threatening those who were watching—came at me from the back. I felt blows on the head, and half-turned and grabbed him by the trousers leg, but he broke away. I tried to grab his legs from under him, and got more blows on the back of the head. I tried to dodge and take them on my shoulders."

P.C. Stone was asked: "Were they blows from a fist?"

"Oh, good Heavens, no," replied the officer. "They sounded metallic. They were much too heavy for fists." Then, he added, a great weight came on him, and he remembered no more until he recovered consciousness in hospital.

Now P.C. Stone did not reveal in court that as he darted across the road he realized that the man with the cosh threatening bystanders was known to him. He knew the man's family as most respectable people and, in fact, this man who struck him so mercilessly from behind, had once been a member of one of his youth clubs, and his father was a personal friend of the officers.

Despite these frightening and most damaging blows P.C. Stone clung tenaciously to the man who had broken the window. By this time a number of people were standing nearby, and they watched as the two men fought with desperation on the pavement.

Most stood stock still, afraid to move because of the menace of the second man with the iron cosh. Then, out of the watching people sprang Mr. D. J. H. Golby, manager of a nearby business. He saw P.C. Stone go for the man at the window, and he saw the "guard" turn to attack him. He immediately, and pluckily, jumped on the "guard's" back. But the guard flung him off and went in to attack P.C. Stone.

Next on the scene with sufficient courage to act came Mrs. Phyllis Holman Richards who was standing on a No. 22 bus preparing to get off when she heard the glass crash, looked up and saw P.C. Stone and the other man fall to the ground fighting.

Mrs. Richards, in her early fifties, saw P.C. Stone and the window-breaker fall to the ground fighting; then she saw the threatening man run up and start hitting the officer on the back of the head "with an instrument somewhat like a truncheon and rather like a hammer." Although at that moment she did not realize that the man being struck was a police-officer she went for the man with the bar.

One of her arms was strapped to her side because of a broken rib, but this did not deter her. She grabbed at the arm wielding the truncheon. The man, shortish, dark, with long black hair, flung her off. Mrs. Richards plunged in again and grabbed him by the waistcoat and heard P.C. Stone call out, "I am a police-officer." She called for help, and went in again to prevent the threatening man strike further blows.

All this time P.C. Stone held on to his man on the pavement and then the threatening man, evidently astonished by the courage and tenacity of Mrs. Richards, pushed her aside and ran to the waiting car, which made off at speed. Then she saw Mr. Herbert Carruthers, managing director of Dibdens, and Mr. Golby go to the aid of P.C. Stone and succeed in overpowering the man who had broken the window.

Further along the road two officers, P.C.s William Warnock and Albert Britton were on plain clothes patrol walking in the direction of Knightsbridge, one on each side of the road. Shortly after 11.45 both saw a crowd gathered further up Sloane Street and, knowing there was a jewellers nearby, both started to run towards it.

As they were running they saw a man run from the direction

of the jewellers and jump into a car which was approaching in their direction. Both had time to see the faces of the driver and passenger, and both noted the registration number of the car.

Note that P.C. Warnock spoke of seeing a "crowd" outside the jewellers, and P.C. Britton said later, "a large number of people." Yet the threatening man, the man who so mercilessly beat P.C. Stone about the head with his weapon, was allowed, apparently, according to all the evidence that can be found, to get past that crowd and enter the getaway car without one person attempting to stop him.

P.C. Graham Summerell was on traffic duty at the Sloan Street junction of Knightsbridge when all this happened, and the first he knew of it was when the conductor of a passing bus told him. He raced to Dibdens and found the window-smasher being held by two civilians. He took hold of him whereupon this villain said, "I've had enough. I'll come quietly. You've got me right. You can find out my name."

The next day, on Wednesday, 18 April, the car in which the other two members of the gang had escaped was found abandoned in Lowndes Place, and two days later the driver, who had been recognized, was arrested in North London, and picked out by P.C.s Warnock and Britton at an identification parade at Gerald Road police station.

Of the third man, the threatening man whom P.C. Stone had recognized, and who had been allowed to escape, there was no sign. After attention at the jewellers, the officer was taken to St. George's Hospital where he remained until 25 April. He was then transferred to Atkinsons Morley Hospital at Wimbledon for an operation on his injured skull. When he left there he went to the Metropolitan Police Nursing Home in Denmark Hill, and such was the seriousness of his injuries that he was not allowed out of bed until 29 May, and then only for half an hour!

Imagine the effect of this brutal attack on the 53-year-old officer. Six months later he was still having medical treatment for headaches and sleeplessness, and he was forced to give up all his private activities such as youth clubs. Then one day he caught sight of the third man standing by a coster's barrow in Brewer Street.

"The effect on me was that everything just went," he said later. "All I could do was phone the police." A month later he again met this gangster in Kennington, and the officer, who in normal times would have tackled him alone and without hesitation, just had to go home and go to bed.

The two men already captured were in July sentenced at the Central Criminal Court to eight years preventive detention and six years imprisonment, but it was not until January 1953 that the third man was captured in Brighton and stood his trial. He, too, was sentenced to eight years imprisonment.

In the meantime, P.C. Stone had retired because of his injuries, and he became security officer at Westminster Hospital —but not before Judges, magistrates, and his colleagues had paid tribute to his magnificently courageous act.

When presenting P.C. Stone with a cheque for £15 from the Reward Fund at Bow Street, in September 1951, the then Chief Magistrate, Sir Lawrence Dunne said, "No more striking example of heroism has ever come before this court." And later, in December, when the officer announced his retirement Mr. Paul Bennett, V.C., said at Marlborough Street, "We are saying good-bye to an old friend and a brave man. He just saw his duty clearly and did it without the slightest hesitation. Had some of the onlookers seen their duty as clearly a third man involved would not have got away."

Nearly every man and woman in the Metropolitan Police Force subscribed to a London Fund for P.C. Stone, and on his retirement he was handed a cheque for £1,690. And in February 1952, it was announced that he had been awarded the George Medal.

For her courage in going to his aid Mrs. Richards was awarded the Binney Medal for 1951 for the bravest civilian act in London in assisting the enforcement of law, and the Committee making the award announced, "Had not Mrs. Richards intervened as she did it is impossible to estimate what the result of this murderous attack might have been." She was the first woman to be awarded the Medal. Mr. Goldby, who also intervened to aid the constable was awarded the Binney Memorial Certificate.

During the January 1953 trial, the third man in his defence denied striking P.C. Stone. All he did, he said, was stand by the getaway car and he lost heart when he saw P.C. Stone come towards him, because he had known the officer for a number of years.

Mr. Justice Byrne told him that he was a dangerous criminal and that he and the second man who wielded a bar to smash the jewellers window were responsible for Mr. Stone's retirement from the police force and his state of health at that time.

Courage in the force, as this story shows, is not confined to any particular age, rank, or section.

What of the public? Time and again we read of thugs beating up police-officers with a crowd watching and no one interfering. Is that the result of fear? Of cowardice? Or of realization that if they do go to the aid of the officer and are hurt they cannot, at the time of writing, expect any compensation?

A White Paper at present before Parliament is expected to rectify this. Claims for compensation should be determined by a judicial body in future. But this is so full of imponderables that it is planned to start it on an experimental basis only.

CHAPTER TEN

UNWELCOME VISITOR

IF the area in which you live is practically free from crime you may be pretty certain that it is largely due to the C.I.D. chief of your nearest police station. He makes it his business, and that of his subordinates, to learn the identities and methods of every criminal living in the district for which he is responsible. And, more often than not, these criminals receive a quite unofficial, but nevertheless stern, warning—"Lay off this manor."

The crook is told that if there is an outbreak of his particular crime in the area he will be the chief suspect; and he will have to give a pretty accurate account of his actions. So the criminal, if he wishes to carry on with his nefarious practises, does so in another district. Close co-operation between the C.I.D. chiefs of every district maintains as far as is possible a check on the movements of these wrongdoers. In a broader sense this prevention of crime movement applies throughout the country, and, indeed, between many countries of the world.

Numerous overseas criminals have found their entry to this country barred either because Scotland Yard knows all about them, or have been informed in advance of their records and impending arrivals. Close and constant watch is kept on all sea and air ports by the Special Branch Officers of Scotland Yard to prevent the entry of such unwanted violators of law and order. Now and again, however, there is a slip up. Such was certainly the case when Justine de Almeida landed at Liverpool from the liner *Hildebrand* on 19 March 1954. For de Almeida was a gunman, and a desperate, dangerous gunman. Yet he carried a legitimate passport as well as a gun when he stepped ashore.

de Almeida, unknown and unsuspected by the immigration officers in Liverpool at that time, had started his life of crime in Massachusetts in 1925 when he was sentenced to from seven to ten years imprisonment for armed robbery. He was pardoned in 1933, but only a month later went to gaol for another two-and-a-half years for being in possession of a gun. In 1937 he was again convicted for armed robbery, and this time was sentenced to twenty-five years imprisonment. After serving six years of this sentence de Almeida was adjudged insane and sent to a mental institution. In 1953 he was paroled and deported to Portugal.

How then was a man with such a menacing record allowed to land freely and openly in this country? The answer is that de Almeida, a Portuguese by birth, had no criminal record in Portugal, and certainly none was recorded here. He went to the British representative in Lisbon, described himself as a commercial traveller, and was given permission, in all good faith, to land in this country on business for a period not to exceed two months.

Just exactly why he did come, why he did bring a gun, why he did murder, will never be known. According to some passengers in the ship he spent a good deal of the voyage locked in his tourist cabin; according to others he spoke of his wife and three children in Lisbon, and told amusing stories of his experiences in America and Portugal. There were also rather vague reports that on one occasion he produced a gun, a .25 Mauser automatic, and muttered veiled threats of a debt he had to pay.

From the moment he landed his movements were enveloped in mystery. No one, in fact, bothered overmuch about the little man who should never have set foot in this country. One thing is certain, however, and that is that de Almeida brought his gun to London.

The first intimation that anything was wrong came on 24 March, only five days after he landed in Liverpool. At about 5.30 p.m. that evening Mr. Walter Kingston went to the small jewellers shop of Wehrles Ltd., in Lisson Grove, Marylebone, to collect a watch he had left there. He found to his surprise that the door was locked.

There was no response to his knocking, and he peered through the glass shop door, and saw by a wall clock in the shop that the time was exactly 5.34. All the lights were on so he rapped again on the door with his keys. He waited for about two minutes then suddenly he heard two cracks. There was a slight pause between each crack, and they sounded, he thought, like the cracking of a whip.

Still puzzled he waited. And about one minute later a woman came running from an alleyway of the cottages alongside the shop. She asked him, "Did you hear those noises in the shop? There have been some loud bangings going on in there. It's very strange, because Mr. Wehrle always puts his shutters up at half past five."

As she finished saying this a girl from the Post Office next door to the Wehrle's shop came out. She, too, said that she had heard strange noises, and with that Mr. Kingston looked through the door again. Then he heard someone thudding against a partition door at the back of the shop.

By this time it was obvious to these people that something was wrong, and the girl from the Post Office wisely decided that it was a matter for police investigation. She ran back to her office to dial 999. In the meantime several other people arrived including one woman who lived in a flat in the cottages.

She ran back to her flat from which she could look into the shop, and within two minutes she returned pale with excitement. "I've had a look from my room, and it looks like two men tied up on the floor at the back of the shop," she said.

Other housewives in Lisson Grove were alerted by the banging noises from the shop. One said to another, "I think they are bashing Mr. Wehrle up." With that they both pluckily ran and banged loudly on the shop door in the hope that the noise they made would frighten the "raiders" away.

While this was going on the Information Room at Scotland Yard received the telephone call from the Post Office girl and sent out a call to police cars 6 "D" and 7 "D" which they knew to be in the area to investigate "unusual noises" coming from a jewellers shop at 39 Lisson Grove.

P.C. Douglas Percy Miller, aged 29, was the wireless operator in 7 "D" and P.C. Leonard Geoffrey Bocking, also 29, the driver. They were very near Lisson Grove and they arrived at the shop at 5.46 p.m.—three minutes after receiving the message. At that time there were twenty to thirty people gathered outside. A moment later car 6 "D" driven by P.C. James Morrison with P.C. George Alexander Sinclair as wireless operator drew up. Within a few seconds the officers heard the story of the whip-like cracks and the banging that had been heard coming from the jewellers shop.

Finding the shop door locked, P.C.s Bocking, Sinclair and Morrison made their way through an alleyway alongside, towards the rear of the shop, leaving P.C. Miller at the front in case the intruder tried to get out that way.

They ran round to Bell Street into the buildings which back onto the rear of the shop, climbed through the bedroom window of one of the flats on to a concrete landing just outside the back door of the shop. Mr. Kingston followed them.

The back door of the shop was open and they went straight in. As soon as they entered they found the proprietor, Mr. Marcus Wehrle, aged 56, lying dead on the floor with a bullet wound between the eyes. Lying beside his body, and at right angles to him, was the jewellers assistant, Mr. Edwards Mansfield, aged 26. He, too, had a bullet wound in the head, and his hands were tied behind his back with a tie around his wrists.

Mr. Mansfield was not dead, but such was his wound that the experienced officers realized there could be little hope for his life. They noted, too, that Mr. Wehrle's tie was missing though he was not bound. Curiously enough there was no sign of any great disorder in the shop. No suggestion that there had been any battle.

It appeared from their brief and first examination that someone had entered the shop at about 5.30, the normal closing time, by the front door which he locked behind him. Apparently he had first held up one man with his gun when he was surprised by the other. He had then forced them both into the workroom at the rear of the premises.

What happened then could only be conjectured. It seemed, however, that he bound the assistant, and was about to bind the proprietor when something happened which caused him cold-bloodedly and deliberately to shoot them both in the head. And it was evident to the shocked officers that the shooting had taken place only a few minutes before their arrival.

Where then was the murderer? He could not have walked out of the front door because of the crowd that had gathered, and because the officers had learned from Mr. Kingston that he had heard the whip-like cracks, evidently the shots *after* he found the front door locked. And he could hardly have escaped from the rear without having been seen by the housewives who had been alerted by the bangings.

P.C. Morrison telephoned for an ambulance and assistance while P.C. Sinclair searched the shop. P.C. Bocking decided to have a look round the yard at the rear of the shop. By this time most of the women in Lisson Cottages, at the rear of the shop were peering from their windows anxious to learn what had happened to the jeweller they all knew so well.

One woman, peering into the yard at the foot of ten stone steps, suddenly saw a man crouching in a corner of the doorway of Epco's, next door to the jewellers. She saw that he was a foreign-looking man, with a dark skin. As she looked down at him he suddenly looked up at her. Then she saw that he had a gun in his left hand. And as he looked up at her he changed the gun from his left to his right hand.

Startled beyond belief the woman shouted to her husband. "There's a man in the yard with a gun." Her husband pulled her away from the window and shut it. At that point P.C. Bocking was standing on the top of the steps with his back to the gunman. The husband of the woman called out to him, "Look out. There's a bloke down there," and pointed to the area basement.

Another housewife who climbed to the top of the flats to see what was going on saw a man crouching in the yard and thought it was Mr. Wehrle, the jeweller, tied up. She shouted out to him and said, "Aid is coming Mr. Wehrle," but the man did not look up. She was surprised that despite repeating her call the man still paid no attention.

By this time P.C. Bocking had turned and as soon as he saw the man crouching in the doorway he called down to him, "What are you doing there?" The man made no reply, and the officer saw him bring up his right hand from beneath the raincoat he was carrying.

Already P.C. Bocking was making his way steadily down the stone steps. He realized immediately that this man was almost certainly the murderer, but he did not waver. His eyes never left the gunman as he moved towards him, step by step. One or two people who could also see the crouching figure shouted a warning that the man had a gun. P.C. Bocking took no notice. So tense was the moment that later he could not clearly recall what he said to the man, or what the petrified onlookers said to him.

When he got to within two or three steps from the bottom, and as he got nearer and nearer, he too saw the gun in the man's right hand. And with that he sprang. He jumped on the crouching man, grabbed his right wrist, and tried to wrestle the gun from him. He knew now he was battling with the killer. But no thought of his own peril entered his head.

Silently the men fought. The officer for his life, and the killer for his freedom. The latter tried desperately to free his gun hand, but P.C. Bocking held on to it with grim determination. As they fought the gun was being waved from side to side in front of the gunman.

After a few moments P.C. Sinclair who had been searching the shop, reached the back door and heard a noise coming from that direction. He went to investigate and saw P.C. Bocking grappling with the man in the area.

He immediately ran down the steps to his colleague's aid. Bocking saw him and shouted a warning, "Look out. He's got a gun." The man was at this time facing P.C. Sinclair, as P.C.

Bocking had grabbed his arms from behind, and the officer saw the gun. Then, just before P.C. Sinclair reached him there was a shot.

Neither P.C.s Bocking nor Sinclair had any idea where the shot went, but the latter did not hesitate. He went straight for the gunman's hand and grabbed the weapon. He tried to wrench it away, but the man clung on to it fiercely. P.C. Sinclair hit him several times in the stomach and eventually pulled the gun away.

P.C. Bocking still held on to the man, and both officers forced him to the ground. As they did so the gunman pulled his right hand away and made for his pocket. P.C. Sinclair saw this, grabbed his hand, and while P.C. Bocking held the gunman down, searched his pockets to see if he had any other weapon.

In the right hand pocket of the raincoat P.C. Sinclair found a brown leather wallet with the initials "M.W." (Marcus Wehrle) on it. And at that moment the gunman suddenly sagged and called out, "I have been shot." Neither officer believed him until P.C. Bocking lifted his shirt and saw a bloodstain on his vest.

They then realized that the shot they had heard in the struggle had entered the man's body. They sent him to St. Mary's Hospital, but he died a few minutes after admission from a bullet wound in the chest. He was soon identified as de Almeida, and at his inquest at St. Pancras on 28 April the jury returned a verdict that he murdered Wehrle and Mansfield, and that his own death was accidental. Mansfield had died in hospital from his wounds on 5 April.

The jury praised the "courageous manner" in which P.C.s Bocking and Sinclair had carried out their duties. Praise well earned indeed, for the gun they wrested from de Almeida was a 6.35 mm. calibre Mauser automatic pistol in good working order from which three bullets had been fired.

Whether or not the shot that killed him was meant for one the officers is one of the many mysteries that remain unsolved regarding de Almeida's first and only visit to this country.

Senior detectives spent hours inquiring into the reason for his visit and the senseless, callous murders of the jeweller and his assistant.

They learned that when de Almeida landed at Liverpool he had about £600 in dollars in his possession. Yet, when he died, he had only £8 18s. 8d. of his own, and no foreign currency. There was £19 in the wallet which he had stolen from Mr. Wehrle. In five days nearly £600 had disappeared. Where?

Was that money brought to pay the "debt" he had talked about? Did he bring it to pay some gang leader with whom he had become entangled? Or did he spend it on one last West End fling, which is far less likely?

Another puzzle that remains unanswered is why he chose to visit Wehrle's shop. de Almeida was an experienced criminal yet he walked into the jewellers' premises when it was obvious that it was still open, that the jeweller and his staff would be about, and that there was bound to be trouble. He had not even bothered to check that the way out at the back would be barred, and that if there was trouble he would be trapped—as he was.

Whatever the answer to these puzzles the heroism of P.C.s Bocking and Sinclair did not go unrecognized, and for their determination to carry out their duty despite the grave risk of being shot dead or disabled both were awarded George Medals.

I understand that senior Yard officers who investigated the shooting held the view that de Almeida walked into the jewellers solely to hold up the staff and steal what he could lay hands on. If that theory is correct one can only surmise that the state of the gunman's mind must have been similar to that of another gunman, a Pole, who ambushed and shot a businessman in the face as he walked to the lift to take him to his office in Victoria Street, Westminster, one morning.

It was on 19 September 1961, and at about 8.55 a.m. Mr. Duncan Charles Tucker, a civil engineer of Mulgrave Road, Cheam, Surrey, a partner in a firm in Victoria Street, was about to enter the lift when there was a sudden blinding flash, and he fell with terrible injuries to the face and eyes.

In the turmoil that followed the gunman escaped. No one saw him, and the Yard detectives who were quickly on the scene headed by Detective-Chief-Inspector Melville Rees, immediately appealed to the public to report if they had seen anyone running from the building shortly before 9 a.m. Inquiries proceeded throughout the day and eventually suspicion for the shooting centred on the Pole, who was employed by the firm as a civil engineer, and who lived at Ebbsfleet Road, Cricklewood.

It appears that the Pole had earlier been employed by British Railways, and became an assistant engineer with them before he left in 1958 when he got it into his head that they were victimizing him. He later worked for the London County Council before joining Mr. Tucker's firm.

At first he was happy, and gave every satisfaction, until in 1960 an official of British Railways called at the firm to discuss bridge work and came, by the sheerest chance, face to face with the Pole who immediately came to the conclusion that his imagined vilification was to start all over again. He brooded silently and alone and eventually decided to bring the matter to light and publicity by shooting one of the partners. He bought a shotgun and lay in ambush, shooting Mr. Tucker from a range of 20 feet—merely because he happened to be the first official to arrive!

Chief-Inspector Rees soon discovered that the Pole was not in his office on the day of the shooting, and further inquiries led him to decide to visit the man's home with two other officers.

At 10 p.m. that night he knocked on the door of the front ground floor room where the Pole lived. It was in darkness and the door was locked. After repeated knocking he heard a voice say, "Who is there? Go away." Rees knocked again and the voice said, "Go away. I won't see you." Rees said, "I am a police-officer. I wish to speak to you. Open the door." He then heard a movement in the room, the light was switched on, and the door unlocked.

Chief-Inspector Rees pushed open the door and found himself staring down the muzzle of a double-barrel sawn-off shot-gun which the Pole was pointing at him.

Chief-Inspector Rees acted instinctively. In an instant he sprang forward, knocked the barrel of the gun down with his forearm, and hit the Pole with a rugger tackle round the waist. The two officers, whom he had ordered to stand a yard or two from the door in case of trouble, came running, and together the three men overcame the Pole, pushed him into a chair and sat on him.

When Rees asked the man, "You know why we are here?" he replied, "Yes, I have been waiting for you. I thought you would come earlier. I had to do it. He was spying for British Railways. If you had not come in two days I would have carried on shooting. It was Tucker because he came first."

In the room the police-officers found cartridges which had been opened and ball bearings inserted to make them more lethal. Chief-Inspector Rees had suspected something of this sort, because he had seen the frightful injuries sustained by Mr. Tucker. It says much for the depth of his courage that despite this he rushed at and disarmed the gunman before he could do any further damage. Later the Pole was found insane and unfit to plead. He was ordered to be detained until the Queen's pleasure be known.

Chief-Inspector Melville Rees, then aged 48, and living in West Acton, was awarded the British Empire Medal for his courage on another working day which quickly changed from routine to highly dangerous.

CHAPTER ELEVEN

FIRST GEORGE CROSS

SENIOR officers at all Metropolitan Police stations have the authority to issue arms to their men if an emergency so demands, but it is rare indeed that it is deemed necessary. It is rarer still that armed officers have found it necessary to use these weapons. Most gunmen are met unexpectedly, and the officer, or officers, deal with them on the spot as did P.C. Bocking and his colleagues.

On one occasion on record, however, such were the circumstances which ensued when two youths were seen to climb to the roof of a warehouse in Croydon, that certain officers were issued with pistols, and one of them found it necessary to use his. It resulted in an epic story of courage and heroism which will certainly always be remembered with pride by the officers of "Z" division who took part.

It happened on the evening of 2 November 1952. Round about 9.20 p.m. Mrs. Edith Ware, of Tamworth Road, Croydon, went to her daughter's bedroom and casually looked out of the window into the road below. After a moment or two the full moon shone through some passing clouds and she saw two men lurking in the shadows of Barlow and Parker's confectionery warehouse on the opposite side of the road.

Their suspicious movements drew her full attention. Then she saw the shorter of the two climb the six-foot high iron grille gate leading into the passageway of the warehouse while the other stood guard on the pavement, looking up and down the road as if he was keeping a look-out. Seconds later, after waiting for a car to pass, this man too climbed the gate, and disappeared into the darkness of the passage.

Mrs. Ware immediately told her husband, and, seconds later, Mr. John William Ware was telling an officer at Croydon police station what his wife had seen. Little did they realize that that call was to spark off a gun battle that fired the imagination of the world in admiration of the cool courage of men of "Z" division.

In the C.I.D. office at Croydon that night sat Detective-Constable Frederick William Fairfax, aged 35, slightly built, 5 ft. 10 in. tall, an ex-captain of the Royal Berkshire Regiment, who had rejoined the Metropolitan Police Force on demobilization. He had been on duty that Sunday, and was nearly due to be relieved and go home to his wife and child when the call came: "Suspects on the roof of Barlow and Parker's warehouse in Tamworth Road, Croydon.

Fairfax was an experienced officer, he had originally joined the Force in 1936, and he set off to investigate with P.C.s Norman Harrison, Claude Raymond Pain and Allen Bercher-Brigden. They travelled by police van, and Fairfax, who took automatic charge, examined the ground floor door and windows of the warehouse, but could find no evidence that the place had been broken into.

Unknown to him at the time the crew of the "Z" wireless car with P.C. Sidney George Miles driving and P.C. James Christie McDonald, as operator, had arrived about the same time. Having examined the ground floor, Fairfax told the three officers with him to take up various positions around the warehouse, while he went to the front of the building, and climbed over the same gate as that which Mrs. Ware had seen the men climb.

As he got over the gate he was told by P.C. McDonald—who had evidently received a later message from the Yard's Information Room—that the two men had climbed one of the drainpipes in the passageway which led to the flat roof of the warehouse. Without any hesitation Fairfax scaled one of the drainpipes. He did not see P.C. McDonald follow him, nor did he know that McDonald being a heavier man was unable to negotiate the last six feet, and had to return.

Fairfax reached the top alone and pulled himself on to the

flat roof. He immediately saw two figures about fifteen to twenty yards away in front of him and to his right. As soon as they saw him they backed away and hid behind a brick lift shaft roof structure. Fairfax walked towards them, and when he was about six feet from the stack he said, "I am a police-officer, come out from behind that stack."

A voice replied, "If you want us—well come and get us."

Fairfax replied, "All right," and with that he dashed behind the stack, grabbed one of the men and pulled him out into the open while the other man ran to the other side of the stack. Until this moment the officer had no idea of the size, age or intentions of the people he was after. There was no way of telling that they were two youths, one aged 19, and the other only 16. All he knew was that two men were on the roof for no good purpose, and it was his duty to arrest them.

In fact the first man that he caught was the elder. Fairfax pulled him from behind the stack with a view to closing in on the other, but as soon as he did so the older boy broke away from him and shouted to his companion, "Let him have it——," mentioning his companion's Christian name.

At that instant there was a flash and a loud report and, said Fairfax later, "I felt something hit my right shoulder which caused me to spin round and fall to the ground. As I got up I saw one man going to the left of me, and the other to the right of me."

Fairfax knew now that one of the youths was armed and prepared to fire. He realized, too, that he had been wounded, but he by no means wavered. He rushed at the man on his right, closed with him, and struck him with his fist, knocking him to the ground. As he did so there was a second report and flash from the other man's gun. Fairfax dropped to the ground, and pulled the man he was holding in front of him as a shield.

Then he pulled this youth—the older one—behind a large skylight, held him down and rubbed one hand over his clothing to discover whether or not he too was carrying a gun. He did not find a gun, but in the right hand coat pocket he found a knuckleduster, and in the right hand breast pocket a dagger.

The young C.I.D. officer now had no doubts about the type of men he was still facing alone. He pocketed the dagger and put on the knuckleduster. The youth he was holding then said, "That's all I've got, Guv'nor. I haven't got a gun." Fairfax said to him, "I'm going to work you around the roof to that doorway over there," pointing to a fire-escape door leading from the roof.

"He will shoot you," replied the youth. Fairfax said nothing in response to this warning. He pushed the youth out in front of him, and worked his way round the roof to the door he had indicated, telling the boy, "If you stand still you should be safe."

In those agonizing minutes with the gunman only a few yards away the wounded detective had acted on his own, but just then he heard P.C. McDonald shout up to him from the passageway below, "I have tried to get up the pipe but can't make it. Can you help me up the last bit?"

Fairfax shouted back, "Yes, I think so," whereupon P.C. McDonald, fully aware of the danger of the gunman, once again climbed the pipe and on this occasion with the help of Fairfax negotiated the last few feet and joined the detective on the roof.

Now that he had reinforcements and one youth safely under control Fairfax shouted to the other to drop his gun.

"Come and get it," replied the gunman defiantly, so Fairfax and McDonald took shelter behind the fire-exit to decide on the next move, handicapped, of course, with the prisoner already in their custody.

McDonald asked Fairfax, "What sort of a gun has he got, Fairy?"

Before the detective could reply the man they held said, "He's got a .45 Colt, and plenty of bloody ammunition for it, too."

Whilst the two officers and their prisoner were sheltering by the roof door McDonald looked out and saw the gunman crouching half-way up a sloping roof beyond the lift shaft, and he saw that he held a gun in his right hand. Then he saw him fire two shots at another officer who had climbed on to a sloping roof.

This was 24-year-old P.C. Harrison who went to the scene with Fairfax in the first place and who, acting on the detective's instructions, had climbed on to the sloping roof above the gunman and Fairfax. He could see them below and he started edging along the roof, twenty-two feet above the ground with his heels in the guttering and lying back on the sloping roof.

When he got about half-way along he saw the gunman approach the edge of the flat roof, look down into Tamworth Road, then look up, and see him. He heard the man say something about "Copper," saw him raise his revolver and fire a shot. Harrison heard the bullet smack into something behind him. Harrison started to edge back towards a chimney stack and the gunman fired at him again. He heard the bullet enter the stack behind him.

Harrison was lucky to get off that roof alive, but he was undaunted. He rushed around the building and joined P.C. Miles who was about to enter the warehouse which had been opened up for them by a member of the staff who arrived with the keys. Both were unarmed. Both knew exactly what they were about to face—a desperate gunman who would not hesitate to shoot.

Back on the roof Fairfax and McDonald held grimly to their prisoner, no doubt planning in their minds how best the gunman could be taken without anyone else being injured. Fairfax knew that his colleagues were stationed about the building, and that further help would have been summoned.

Just then they heard their colleagues call from the door—it was Miles and Harrison—and Fairfax shouted to them that he was to the right of the door and the man with the gun was to their left. Miles was ahead of Harrison. He kicked the roof door open, and burst through. But even as he jumped there was a loud report and Fairfax, McDonald and Harrison were shocked to see their colleague, P.C. Miles, aged 42, an officer with 22 years service in the force, slump to the ground.

Miles did not get up. He lay there on the roof in full view of the gunman. Fairfax and McDonald, regardless of their peril, unheeding of their own safety, immediately broke cover and ran to his aid.

Even as they did so they heard another shot as the gunman fired again. But they paid no heed. Fairfax dropped on one knee beside P.C. Miles and caught him by the shoulders. McDonald caught hold of his legs and together they dragged him behind the fire-escape. Hastily Detective Fairfax examined him, but P.C. Miles was already beyond human aid. He had been shot dead between the eyes.

P.C. Harrison, who was immediately behind Miles, looked out and saw the gunman again raise the revolver in his two hands and fire. He heard the bullet hit the brickwork of the doorway. Harrison leaned out of the doorway and threw his truncheon, a bottle of milk and a block of wood—the only weapons he could find—at him.

Then he heard the gunman shout, naming himself, and adding, "Come on you coppers, I'm only 16."

Then, despite the fact that he was in full view of the gunman P.C. Harrison, aged 24, and with only just over two years service in the force, leapt from the doorway and joined Fairfax and McDonald.

There is no record of what discussion passed between Fairfax and McDonald when they found that P.C. Miles had been killed, but as soon as the roof door had been opened and they were joined by Harrison, Detective Fairfax who, despite his wound, was still in complete command, decided on his next course of action.

He decided to get the prisoner they still held out of the way so that they could concentrate all their efforts on catching the gunman. After a moments discussion he and Harrison jumped out and pushed their man ahead of them towards the doorway. Fairfax went through the door first, and as Harrison pushed the boy towards him they heard him shout to the gunman, "—— they're taking me down." They heard the young gunman call back, "Are they hurting you ——?"

By this time, as was expected, the officers Fairfax had

stationed around the warehouse and who had heard the shooting, had sent for reinforcements. These had arrived there just as Fairfax and Harrison led their prisoner down the stairs, and they handed him over to them.

Some of these officers, on the authority of the senior officer on duty at Croydon police station at that time, had been issued with arms, and one of these handed Detective-Constable Fairfax a pistol.

Once again, without any thought of his own personal danger, Fairfax ran up the staircase to the roof door and shouted to the gunman, "Drop your gun, I also have a gun."

He heard the gunman reply, "Come on then, Copper, let's have it out."

With that Fairfax jumped from the doorway where only a few minutes earlier he had seen a brother officer shot dead. As he did so he heard another shot come from the darkness of the roof, but he did not falter.

The full moon flickered through the passing clouds as this courageous officer ran in a semi-circle towards the gunman firing his pistol as he ran. He was running in the face of a gun held by a youth who had already wounded him and killed one of his colleagues. He was running, fully aware of his grave danger. He was alone on the roof with a killer.

A few moments earlier P.C. Robert James William Jaggs, aged 28, one of the reinforcements who had arrived, had decided to climb on to the roof by way of the drainpipe that Fairfax had used earlier. And as he neared the top he heard the gunman's weapon click a time or two as if he was trying to fire, but the weapon was empty.

Then he and Fairfax heard the gunman shout, "Give my love to ——," mentioning a girl's name, and they saw him turn and dive off the roof, head first, into a garden twenty-two feet below. He landed at the feet of one of the officers on guard round the warehouse, and despite the fall, was still conscious. This officer heard him say, "I wish I was —— dead. I hope I have killed a —— lot."

Fairfax went down to the street and into the garden where

the gunman had fallen. Officers lifted the injured youth over the roof of a shed and carried him to an ambulance. Fairfax went with him to Croydon General Hospital where both received treatment. As Fairfax took off his jacket for the medical examination the bullet which had struck him fell from it. He had a searing wound in the region of his right collar bone—but the bullet did not penetrate his skin, and there was no fracture.

The gunman was found to be suffering from a fractured left wrist, a fractured spine and contusion of the chest. He threw his revolver just as he dived off the roof, and this was found later —a .45 Colt with the barrel sawn off—in a greenhouse near the spot where he fell. It contained four spent cartridges and two unspent. Three spent cartridges were later found on the floor of the roof.

The gunman, the boy aged 16, was in hospital for some time before he was able to attend court where with the boy aged 19 he was charged with the murder of P.C. Miles, and the attempted murder of Detective-Constable Fairfax. At their trial in December the case for the Crown was that the younger boy had wilfully murdered P.C. Miles, and that the elder boy had incited him to begin the shooting, and although technically under arrest at the actual time of the killing he was party to the murder, and equally responsible in law.

It emerged that the two young men had known each other in their schooldays, and although their parents had made efforts to stop them going out together, they still did so. The younger boy, it was stated, had never managed to read or write because he suffered from "word blindness." He, it was said, began to be interested in guns when he was aged only 11, and in November 1951, about twelve months earlier, had been fined at Hove for being in unlawful possession of a revolver.

On the night of the shooting of P.C. Miles the two boys had met, and together caught a bus to West Croydon. They walked to Tamworth Road and climbed the drainpipe on to the flat roof of the warehouse unaware, of course, that by the merest chance that she was visiting her daughter's bedroom at that same moment, they had been seen by Mrs. Ware. Shortly after

E

they arrived on the roof, however, they saw a torch shine in a garden below, and realized the police were after them.

Before the trial detectives went to the home of the younger boy, and there they found, hidden under some floor boards, a piece of the sawn off barrel from the revolver he used, as well as a vast array of ammunition.

Yet this boy was not hanged for the murder for which he was found guilty. Because of his age he was ordered to be detained during Her Majesty's pleasure. The elder boy, the boy who had no gun, was hanged.

At the conclusion of the trial of these youths, Lord Goddard, then the Lord Chief Justice, called Fairfax, McDonald and Harrison to the well of the court at the Old Bailey and said, "The conduct of the men of "Z" division on this night in arresting these two desperate young criminals is worthy of the highest commendation, and of the thanks of the community to the police for their gallant conduct.

"It is no light thing to face a burglar or a housebreaker in the dark when he is firing a revolver in the way these two men did. No doubt all the police-officers showed courage that night. They are all deserving of commendation, but I think it is these three officers in particular who were exposed to the worst, and had more opportunity to show their courage and resolution. The thanks of all law-abiding citizens ought to be given to you."

This tribute from the Lord Chief Justice was followed by an announcement in January 1953, that Detective-Constable Fairfax had been awarded the George Cross—the first serving officer to be so honoured.

P.C. Harrison and P.C. McDonald were awarded George Medals, and P.C. Miles, who was killed, the King's Police Medal, posthumously. P.C. Robert James William Jaggs, aged 28, received the British Empire Medal.

Typical of the modesty of hero Fairfax was his reply when later the officers assembled at Croydon to receive the congratulations of Sir Harold Scott, then the Metropolitan Police Commissioner.

It was an occasion of both pride and sorrow, he said—

sorrow that their pal Miles could not be there. "I do not look upon these as individual awards but awards that have been made on behalf of all our colleagues in "Z" division."

The official citation said that the officers "Acted in the highest tradition of the Metropolitan Police Force and gave no thought to their own safety in their efforts to arrest armed and dangerous criminals. Detective Sergeant Fairfax—he was promoted to Detective-Sergeant a month after the gunfight—repeatedly risked death or serious injury, and although wounded did not give up until the criminals were safely in charge of the police."

His heroism echoed round the world, and he had hundreds of letters of praise and congratulations from police and private individuals, while an Italian magazine front-paged a dramatic artists impression of the scene on the Croydon rooftop with Fairfax standing beside the body of P.C. Miles facing the bullets of the gunman.

Later, however, he received a number of anonymous letters and telephone calls threatening death. They were obviously from the criminal underworld or from cranks and for a time all calls and letters were intercepted to save him further annoyance; and unknown to him special watch was kept on his home in Selsdon, Surrey.

On 17 February 1953, Fairfax and his colleagues went to Buckingham Palace and there, in the white and gold State ballroom the Queen pinned to the lapel of his morning coat the George Cross, and told him she wanted to hear from his own lips just what happened.

On his promotion to Detective-Sergeant Fairfax was posted to West End Central police station but in April 1953 he was posted back to Croydon and remained there until his retirement in 1962. After 25 years service in the police he opened a tobacconist and confectionery business in Shirley, Surrey. More recently, however, he gave up this business, and moved to another address with an ex-directory telephone number to save being bothered by many who will never forget his courageous leadership in the rooftop gun battle which many senior officers at the Yard still regard as an epic of heroism rarely, if ever, surpassed in the history of the Metropolitan Police.

Every other officer who took part in that battle was commended. It was not forgotten that they were deployed at strategic points, round the warehouse, and were at all times within range of the gunman. Every man stood fast to his post with calm determination and unflinching courage.

They, besides those already mentioned, included: P.C.s Charles Henry Northeart, Daniel Victor Wells, Edward William Roberts, Henry George Stevens, James Leslie Alderson, Douglas Henry Barrow, Gordon Morrison Stewart, Norman Mitchell, Arthur Basil Church, Walter Edward Carey, Henry William Trevor Harris, Stuart Stanley Lowe, Leslie Moore, James Cobbam Gordon, Harry Fenwick, and James Locke Ross; Inspectors Thomas Foster Bodley and Charles Edward Cook, and Woman-Constable Lilian Collis.

CHAPTER TWELVE

CIVILIAN AID

THE possibility of gaol is always well in the mind of habitual criminals. It is an occupational hazard. If they win they have a soft life, easy money and lots of leisure. If they lose it is gaol where money has no meaning, and most of the leisure hours are spent behind bars. Their reaction to being trapped varies. It is when they are in possession of guns that they are the most dangerous.

And guns are still far too easily come by. If you have one in your home at this moment take heed of this story, and what happened when a young desperado broke into a house in Stamford Hill one night and found a loaded revolver, and a number of spare bullets. He had led a life of crime from the age of 14, but now at the age of 20, he was, for the first time, in possession of a gun.

The incidents which immediately preceded his using the gun started towards the end of August 1950, when he met two other criminals in a cafe in Aldgate. These two had earlier stolen some cameras in Bethnal Green Road, and hidden them in a bombed site in the area. Now they wanted some assistance in getting rid of them. The three crooks went to the site, picked up the cameras, and were walking with them in a carrier bag along Brick Lane when they were stopped by two alert policemen.

The officers asked what was in the carrier bag and were told, "Some books." These three men did not look in the least the types that would spend their leisure hours in reading, and when the officers demanded to look in the bag, our 20-year-old criminal decided to bolt. He had already handed up his identity card, realized that the officers would soon have his record, so he didn't stop bolting until he arrived at the hopfields in Yalding, Kent.

He worked on a farm for a couple of weeks, until he thought the heat of the search for him would be off, and, disliking work of any description anyway, he returned to Aldgate, sleeping out. Money became scarce, and the time arrived that made another job a necessity. That was when he found the house in Stamford Hill.

After satisfying himself that the occupants were out he forced a window from the front garden and entered a bedroom. In one of the wardrobes he found a cash box with £15 in notes and some silver, and the loaded revolver with spare bullets lying beside it. He was not disturbed in any way, and he returned to Aldgate hanging about cafes waiting for the next easy touch to turn up.

On Monday, 25 September, another 20-year-old criminal set out to find him, and that night the two met at the Elephant and Castle. They had known each other for some years and decided to team up. They slept rough, and wandered round the East End just looking for the opportunity to thieve.

On the morning of the 27th of September, between 11 a.m. and 11.30 a.m., they went to a block of buildings in Bethnal Green where they had been told a rent collector would be at work, and that if they timed their attack correctly he would be carrying about £200. They arranged to waylay him on one of the landings of the building, and that either one of them, who- ever was nearest, would punch him on the jaw, lay him out, and take the cash.

The fact that he might be an elderly man, and that their attack might easily cause him permanent injury never even occurred to them. All they bothered about was that here, ap- parently, was an "easy touch," a rent collector on his own, and they were two to one. They did not take into account that East End rent collectors are fully aware of the risks they run at the hands of such thugs, and are constantly on the alert for them.

When they arrived at the block of buildings in Old Nichol Street they soon saw the rent collector approaching. Both made for him, but he spotted them, realized that something was wrong, and before either could land a telling blow, he ducked and ran away. The two thugs saw £200 slipping from their grasp so they gave chase.

One of them caught up with him and hit him. In the struggle to free himself and escape the collector spilled some silver and copper from the leather money bag he carried over his shoulder, but he managed to wriggle free and ran back into one of the buildings where he had earlier been collecting rents. He was shouting for help, and creating such a commotion that three dogs started to attack him, but the thugs still went after him, kicking out at the dogs until people in the flats came to the rent man's rescue.

The two bandits then beat a retreat, picking up some of the silver that had been dropped as they ran. That attack yielded only about four half-crowns and two two-shilling pieces instead of the £200 they expected. They bolted off through some back turnings in the area, and went to their usual haunts, the cafes frequented by criminals of their own calibre.

Later that afternoon they walked around the East End looking for a likely place to break into. Money was short, but they never dreamed of looking for a job. Anyone who showed any signs of money that afternoon was in danger. But no one did, and neither man was sufficiently familiar with the business premises to suggest any as a likely spot to break into.

Then, about 7 p.m. that evening, the second of the two 20-year-old thieves who had at one time lived at Keston, and knew the area well, suggested that they should go to Biggin Hill. He told his companion that he knew a number of likely places in the area that they could "do." So they set off by Green Line bus, and arrived there at about 10 p.m.

As is usual with such types their first call was at a public house. They needed a drink, but that was not the main object of their call. They wanted to see who was about. Whether there were any inquisitive detectives they might recognize. Or any other criminals who might have decided on action in the same area.

They had two or three drinks, and then the second man remembered Temples Stores which, he said, "sold everything," and should be quite easy to "do." He was referring to Temples Limited, general storekeepers, at the junction of Stock Hill and Hillcrest Road, and the two of them walked there. As soon as his companion looked through the windows of the stores he agreed that this was the place suitable for their operation.

Keeping their eyes open for any passersby they made their way round to the back of the premises, but they saw no suitable way of breaking in, so they went to the side of the building. There, they climbed over a flat roof, and into a small courtyard where they smashed a hole in a window and climbed in.

Completely unknown to them that action set off a hidden burglar alarm, the bell of which rang in the room of Mr. Thomas Temple, a director of the company, who was sleeping in a house adjoining the stores. He got out of bed, looked through his window, and saw enough to confirm the alarm warning that there were intruders in the store. He immediately telephoned Farnborough police station who flashed his message to Scotland Yard's Information Room.

This is exactly the sort of action that delights the police. The kind of co-operation they yearn. In short, "Don't do anything yourself. Warn us first." As events proved it was just as well that Mr. Temple made no attempt to tackle the intruders on his own, although, of course, he had no idea at that time that one of them was carrying a loaded revolver—the revolver stolen from the house in Stamford Hill.

Mr. Temple, who was 53, then telephoned his son and two relatives who lived nearby. Then he dressed and walked out to the store where he arrived just in time to see a police car draw quietly up. Police-Constables John McCallum, the driver, Owen Percival Ashwin, the wireless operator, and Ivan King, the observer, in car 8 "P" had received the Yard's message "suspects on the premises" at 12.51 a.m., and had arrived at the store within two minutes!

As they held a brief conference with Mr. Temple on their plan of action the two criminals inside were moving about quietly pocketing anything they could find worth while. The first—the one with the gun—took two pens from a drawer. The second found a cheque. They pulled all the drawers from a desk before mounting a flight of stairs to an office above.

Here they found a safe which they ransacked. A tin collecting box for the Biggin Hill War Memorial Fund, and three collecting stockings for the Greater London Fund for the Blind, were opened, and all the cash taken. These thieves didn't care who went short as long as they could get cash or articles that could easily be turned into cash. Completely unaware of what was happening outside they pilfered this and that and . . . then suddenly the lights went on.

Mr. Temple, when he met the three constables outside told them, "They are still inside. If one of you will come with me I will switch the lights on." P.C. Ashwin, aged 45, and within one month of 20 years service with the police, decided to go with Mr. Temple while P.C. McCallum also aged 45, and P.C. King, aged 25, took up vantage points outside in case the suspects attempted to break out.

Mr. Temple and P.C. Ashwin went to the back of the building, unlocked the back door, locked it behind them, and switched on the lights. They separated, and crept quietly into the main building by two different staircases. As the former approached the offices, he was rejoined by the constable, and both saw two men inside the office which had glass panels.

P.C. Ashwin first saw the fair hair on a man's head. Then the man stood up, pointed a gun which he held in his right hand at the officer and fired. The shot missed both him and Mr. Temple, who was standing just behind him, and immediately the two thieves bolted from the office door, turned right along a corridor, and disappeared from view.

The two men gave chase into a clothing room at the rear of the building and here, P.C. Ashwin who was leading, came face to face with the smaller of the two men (the one without a gun) and immediately closed with him. As they battled for mastery the gunman stood with his back to a staircase which led into the clothing room and fired again, this time at the officer who was struggling with his confederate. Then he turned the gun and aimed one shot at Mr. Temple.

P.C. Ashwin felt something strike him near the throat just as he and the man he was holding fell to the floor. Then he lost consciousness. He remembered no more.

The gunman ran down the staircase, and as Mr. Temple made to follow him, he heard a plate glass window smash. Believing that the bandit had jumped through the window, and knowing that two officers and possibly some of the relatives he had warned were outside in case that happened, he returned to go to the assistance of P.C. Ashwin.

He found the wounded officer lying on the floor with the robber on top of him shouting, "Come on, Bill, I have got the bastard."

Mr. Temple had armed himself with a wooden batten, and he ran up to the young thug and struck him about the head as hard as he could. He laid about the man so effectively that on about the third stroke the batten broke and the crook yelled, "Don't, Guv-nor. I ain't got a revolver."

Mr. Temple, his 53 years of courage and determination having won, ordered the 20-year-old thug to stand up, put his hands on his head, and stand in a corner where he could keep an eye on him. Then he tried to arouse P.C. Ashwin, and was rendering him what aid he could until help arived.

Meanwhile outside the building his relatives had arrived, and were assisting P.C.s McCallum and King in guarding exits from the store when they heard the shots. P.C. King climbed to the roof of a building as he thought there might be a skylight through which the men might try to escape. Just as he got to the roof he heard a crash of glass below him and he saw the gunman emerge from the smashed window with a revolver in his right hand.

Mr. Reginald Alfred Temple, aged 52, a brother of Mr. Thomas Temple, was patrolling between Stock Hill and Hillcrest Road when he heard four or five shots inside the store. He looked towards the furnishing department, and saw a man inside pick up a wooden display stand, and smash the window with it. Then the man jumped through the hole he had made.

Mr. Reginald Temple ran towards him and grabbed one of his wrists, but the man turned, pushed a revolver in his chest, and broke free running into Hillcrest Road.

P.C. McCallum was only a few yards away, and he too made a grab at the fleeing gunman but failed to get hold of him properly. The officer chased after him in the darkness and was soon joined by P.C. King who had leapt from the roof as soon as he realized what was happening. When P.C. King caught up with him McCallum shouted to him that the man still had a gun.

The chase went on for 400 yards or so with the officers gradually gaining, then suddenly the gunman stopped, turned, pointed the gun at P.C. McCallum who was only five feet away from him, and shouted, "I've got a gun. This is your lot."

Both officers then distinctly heard the gun click as the trigger was pulled, but neither hesitated. McCallum jumped for the right hand and got hold of the gun. King jumped to the left and got hold of the left arm. There was a violent struggle but the gunman was no match for the two officers, and after a few minutes he was overpowered. When they took him back to the car and searched him they found seven rounds of .25 ammunition.

P.C. McCallum stayed with the prisoner while P.C. King entered the store. He found P.C. Ashwin lying on the floor behind a showcase. He saw that he was having difficulty in breathing, so he opened his tunic and shirt front, and saw that he had been shot in the base of the neck. A local doctor was summoned and P.C. Ashwin was admitted to Farnborough Hospital in a critical condition. He was, in fact, still in hospital in November of that year when the two young thugs appeared for their trial at Kent Assizes at Maidstone. The gunman, who was described by Mr. Justice Humphreys as "a desperado" was sentenced to fourteen years imprisonment, and his accomplice to five years.

The gunman, as has been said, had been a criminal from

boyhood. He had 13 convictions before the shooting—"Assault with intent to rob"—"Wounding with intent to resist arrest"—"Robbery with violence." Said Mr. Justice Humphreys when passing sentence on him, "You shot at a police-officer and you very nearly committed murder. You shot him in the chest; he was very, very ill and might well have died. It is no thanks to you that you are not now being charged with the crime of wilful murder. And if you had been you would have had no sort of defence. You were caught redhanded."

He admitted that he had fired all five bullets in the gun, and it was empty when McCallum and King caught him. It was, fortunately for them, empty when he aimed it at them and pulled the trigger. Yet what effect did this experience and his sentence have on him? He turned to the judge and sneered, "Thanks, Judge. Aren't you generous?"

There is no doubt that the Judge's description of him as "a desperado" was most apt, yet there is no record that he had ever used a gun before that day he broke into the house at Stamford Hill. Maybe the owner of that house had a legal right to the gun, and a good reason for keeping it. Maybe it was just a war souvenir.

But the fact that it was kept loaded, with more ammunition nearby, and in an easily accessible spot, very nearly led to the murder of a police-officer. No greater emphasis could be laid on the danger of having weapons about the house. No home is safe when the occupants are out, and if guns have to be kept they should be under lock and key at all times that the owner has no personal supervision of them.

The bullet which hit P.C. Ashwin just above the breastbone lodged in the muscles of the right side of his back, and caused severe damage to the right lung. For some time his condition was regarded as "very serious." His neighbours at St. Mary Cray, Kent, prayed for him, and his wife was given a bed in hospital during the critical days so that she could be near him. Never once did she miss a daily visit to her husband for five weeks.

He was not discharged from hospital until 3 December and

was on sick leave until he was allowed to resume light duty on 15 January. After a while, however, he went back to his old love—patrol cars—and he carried on helping to look after homes, and offices, and warehouses, and people, until his retirement in November 1959.

Before his retirement, however, the courage of P.C. Ashwin, and his colleagues McCallum and King, were officially recognized. All three were awarded George Medals together with Mr. Thomas Temple, the director of the company, for his outstanding courage in facing the gunman, and so ably dealing with the second bandit who was attacking the wounded officer.

For his fine example of active support to the police in their war against crime Mr. Temple was also awarded the Binney Medal for 1950. There could scarcely be a better example of co-operation than that he gave that September night, or a finer demonstration of the fearlessness of the police in tackling an armed and extremely dangerous man who, by accident, had obtained possession of a gun.

This desperado refused to behave even in prison. In December 1952, he was given twelve strokes of the cat-o'-nine tails for attacking a warder with an iron bar. For that assault he also lost 12 months remission of sentence, and had 13 days on No. 1 punishment—bread and water only for meals.

Even this punishment was not enough. Only four months later he broke away in the exercise yard of the prison, and, with two other convicts, climbed to the roof of a cell block and flung slates and stones at warders below. Only when warders turned hoses on the three did they force them to surrender, wet and exhausted, after ninety minutes.

I do not recall any occasion where an officer has been shot and the Metropolitan Police have failed to find, and arrest the gunman. They realize the potential, frightening danger of such a man, and know that he will almost certainly shoot again to resist arrest, and the consequent long term of imprisonment.

This desperado is one of many who haunt the streets of the Metropolis beating up old men and women or anyone else who stands in their way of robbery. Violence is their password and, in many cases, guns their weapons. The Yard men never know when, or in what circumstances, they will meet these gangsters.

They are aware that any call at any time of the day or night might result in gunplay or violence and they are always ready for it. Particularly so if suspects are reported in the premises of a gunsmith as happened early one morning in May 1948, when they found themselves dealing with an incident, led by another desperado who proved equally as villainous and dangerous as that dealt with by P.C.s Ashwin, McCallum and King.

It was shortly after 4 a.m. on that Saturday morning in May that Police-Sergeant Ralph Sheppard in a police patrol car with P.C. Henry Paterson Kay driving, was ordered to investigate a report that suspects had entered the premises of Cogswell and Harrison Ltd., gun makers, in Park Road, East Acton.

They raced through the darkened streets and arrived there within a few minutes. Sergeant Sheppard decided to enter the factory, and ordered P.C. Kay and P.C. William Tween, the observer, to remain on guard outside in case the suspects tried to make a break.

He walked quietly through the building and suddenly surprised the youths, one with an oxy-acetylene torch, bending over a safe they were trying to burn open. As soon as they saw him, the elder boy who held the torch flung it at the officer then turned and bolted. In fact, though Sergeant Sheppard was not aware of it at the time, these youths aged 19 and 18 had a third partner, a boy of 15½, but he was not in sight at the time.

The sergeant gave chase, and then as the elder of the two youths reached two steps leading from the room, he turned, produced a gun and said, "Keep back, or I'll shoot you." Sergeant Sheppard replied by seizing a hammer which was lying on a ledge beside him and throwing it at the gunman. Then he shouted a warning to Kay, "They are armed, Jock." He then jumped sideways to avoid a possible shot, but tripped and fell over the safe. While he was still down the gunman pointed the gun at him and said, "Keep out of this—right out, or I'll kill you."

Then the gunman disappeared, and the sergeant in following him came across the second youth. He chased him over several gardens, caught him, and, after a short struggle overpowered him. "I've had enough," said the youth. "You are choking me. Look at my suit." This 18-year-old did not have a gun, but a quantity of ammunition was found on him.

Meanwhile P.C. Kay, aged 39, a married man with two children, had seen the men breaking out, and he shouted a warning to P.C. Tween, "Look out, Bill they are coming out. They have got guns." With that he drew his truncheon, kicked open the gate of a shed where the gunman had fled, and walked in—in the face of a gun.

As he walked towards the gunman there was a bang and he fell to the ground. P.C. Tween heard the gunman say, "Take that you ——," and then the desperado went out through the shed, and onto the roof of it.

A few minutes later the roof of the wooden shed on which he stood in defiance cracked ominously. He jumped down, stumbled, and the gun fell from his hand. Sergeant Sheppard, who had by this time returned, and P.C. Tween, were on him in a flash, both wielding their truncheons. The young desperado put up a desperate fight but was eventually overpowered. The 15½-year-old-boy was caught later.

All three appeared at the Old Bailey in June 1948, and the gunman was sentenced to five years penal servitude for shooting at P.C. Kay with intent to resist arrest. The bullet which hit the officer lodged in his hip-bone and, it was said at the time, would probably stay there the rest of his life. The 18-year-old boy was sent to Borstal for a period not exceeding three years, and the 15½ went to an approved school.

Mr. Justice Birkett imposing these sentences said, "The police of this country are engaged in the protection of the citizens' rights, their property and their person, and no State can permit for one moment that men who are so engaged shall suffer attack, and murderous attack, of the kind that took place that night. The police-officers in this case are worthy of the highest possible commendation, particularly P.C. Kay. I hope very much their meritorious and gallant conduct will be brought to the notice of the proper authority."

It was. Both Sergeant Sheppard and P.C. Kay were awarded the King's Police Medal for Bravery in their dealing with another gunman whose sentence by no means resulted in the end of his conflict with law and order. This local boy from Acton planned and initiated that escapade at Acton, and had not long served his sentence when he was in trouble again.

He received another five years at Worcester for office-breaking and larceny, and this time was sent to the dreaded Dartmoor Gaol. Here he was in touch with two other notorious gunmen—a Hammersmith man who shot at the Beadle of Burlington Arcade in 1959, and was serving ten years, and a Shoreditch man who was serving fifteen years for a series of dreadful offences in the Midlands which involved shooting a man in the thigh, and beating a police-officer on the head with a pistol.

This trio planned, and took part in, one of the most audacious ever escapes from the Moor in June 1963. They ran from the exercise yard, and boarded a ten-ton tanker that had just finished unloading fuel oil at the prison and, with the Acton man driving, made off towards the front gate. The other gunmen beat off warders who attempted to jump on the vehicle.

They hit a wall, but then drove round the walls until they came to metal-sheathed back gates which were shut. The Acton gunman crashed the tanker straight through them, and continued down a narrow lane and across fields on to the main road. Here they abandoned the tanker and flagged down a car that happened to be passing.

The driver, unaware of what had happened, thought there had been an accident, and stopped. The gangsters bundled him out of his car and drove off. They abandoned this car later knowing full well that all roads over a wide area would be sealed. The Acton man separated from the others in the Widecombe area, about eight miles from the prison, but all three were recaptured in about nine hours. And each was sentenced to a further fifteen months imprisonment.

The first boy had been in trouble with the police since the age of 14; the second from the age of 12. What can be done to reform them is a problem that has not yet been solved. Prison in its present state does not seem to.

CHAPTER THIRTEEN

TROUBLE FROM TRIVIA

IT is astonishing how some trivial incident, some minor misdemeanour of comparative little importance, may, in the warped mind of a criminal, develop beyond all reason. This happens especially when the man concerned has made a temporary success of his thieving activities, as he sometimes does, and he then has money to burn, which he invariably does. Such eruptions into major crime occur especially when the person concerned is foolish enough to carry a gun.

In October 1946, a 27-year-old London man, a man with a list of 14 convictions for crime in which he had indulged from the age of 16, deserted from the Army, and returned to what he considered the easier life of crime. Within two months he had made it pay and pay handsomely. He broke into at least forty-four houses in the Walton, Weybridge and Horsham areas, and he literally had money to burn.

Like almost every known criminal of his type it was easy come, easy go. He robbed at night, and lived a life of luxury and ease during the day. He ate well and drank far too much, but he didn't care; and by the Christmas of that year his pockets were well-lined with his ill-gotten gains.

He realized that the police and the military authorities were looking for him, but they were looking for many other deserters, too, and he felt reasonably safe as long as he did nothing foolish in the day-time, such as getting drunk, and drawing attention to himself. He had studied the Walton-Weybridge areas well, and reckoned his chances of getting caught during his nefarious practises there were worth the risk. And anyway, just in case just to be on the safe side, he carried a gun.

Exactly why he carried the gun no one knows. It may have been to frighten any householder who disturbed him robbing his home, or it may have been to resist arrest. But the Browning automatic was with him night and day, and on Christmas Eve of that year when he decided to celebrate in the West End of London he carried it, fully loaded, in his pocket.

He made his way to Soho where he knew he would meet men of his own calibre and women of the type that he sought to join with him in celebration. He wandered from pub to pub, never staying too long, nor spending too much, in one; and he was careful never to flash the large roll of notes he carried.

Eventually when he had drunk a fair amount of liquor he fell into conversation with a young blonde woman who took his fancy. The fact that she was already accompanied by a man apparently did not matter to any one of them. They drank together and toasted many merry Christmases together until closing time. Then all three decided that they needed something to eat. Everything was going well for the deserter. All was working exactly as he planned, and the blonde had made it clear that she had no intention of leaving him that night.

So he was full of good humour when they walked together to a cafe in New Cavendish Street, entered, and sat at a table. There was a large number of coloured airmen and soldiers in the cafe, and there was some delay in the service with the result that the deserter, now admittedly two-thirds drunk, became very impatient. He watched the waitress with an ever-mounting anger, and then came what was for him the final straw.

He formulated the idea that the waitress had picked up his knife, fork and spoon in order to serve a coloured man first, and he went out of his mind. He rose to his unsteady feet, and swung a fist at the waitress, hitting her on the chin. She fell, back, and for the moment there was pandemonium.

Then several coloured men, astounded at what they had seen, rushed over to the deserter crook, got hold of him, and flung him from the cafe. There is little doubt that he received some blows in the process, but, according to his own story later, the coloured men gave him such a "good beating up" that he shammed unconsciousness, and fell to the pavement.

When he jumped up and ran off a number of coloured men still stood outside the door of the cafe. Also in the vicinity were the man and the blonde woman who had accompanied him there. They thought the incident was over. It was now just after midnight. Christmas Day, the day of peace and goodwill, had dawned.

But not so for the maddened and frustrated deserter. After he had run a few yards, he turned, produced his loaded revolver, and ran back towards the cafe, firing as he came. Aloysius Abbott, a 22-year-old Jamaican aircraftsman, who was among the men outside the cafe, was hit twice in the chest, and fell dead.

The deserter gunman fired more shots but, luckily, no one was hit. He then found himself near the blonde girl he had met earlier, and, pushing her ahead of him, he ran from the startled crowd still with the revolver held menacingly in his hand.

When they turned the first corner out of sight of the cafe the two slowed down to a walk, so as not to attract attention, and made their way to a hotel in the vicinity of Russell Square where they registered, under false names, as man and wife. In the hotel bedroom the girl was terrified when the man again produced the gun and laid it on the bed; but she did nothing about it.

A few minutes later she went to the bathroom. On returning she saw him fiddling with the gun. Then suddenly there was an explosion, and a bullet entered the bed on which he was sitting. It was then that he told the blonde that he would have fired more shots outside the cafe, but the gun had jammed.

Still the girl did nothing. They went to bed, and next morning read in the newspapers of the death by shooting of the young Jamaican. "Don't worry," he said to the girl. "If I get caught I shan't be caught alive. I will shoot it out." Still the girl did nothing.

They remained at the hotel together until the 27th of December then, for some reason known only to themselves, decided to part. In the meantime, of course, every officer in the West End was on the look-out for the gunman. They had been given a good description of him by those who had seen the shooting, and they realized that he was probably still in the company of the blonde who had also been well described.

At 11.30 a.m. on the 27th they left the hotel together, and were walking along towards a Tube station, and were in Tavistock Place when they were spotted by Police-Constables B. J. (Bertie) Rowsell and Norman Strange, both in plain clothes, both acting as *aides* to the C.I.D. Both knew of the shooting incident outside the cafe on Christmas Day, and both thought the man and his blonde companion answered the descriptions of those the police wanted to see.

The moment the deserter-gunman had dreaded arrived. The officers stood in his path, said they were police-officers and asked, "May we see your identity card, please?" His reply was immediate. He pulled the gun from his pocket, rammed it into the stomach of P.C. Strange and said, "Don't come another inch or I'll ram your guts in."

Then he turned and bolted. Both officers immediately gave chase, one commandeering a taxi, and the other a passing van. The gunman ran towards the Underground station but found too many people in the way, so he turned and ran round a block of buildings.

On one occasion the taxi got very near, so he turned and fired a shot at it. By this time hundreds of people round about Tavistock Place, Cartwright Gardens and Marchmont Street realized what was happening, and they watched, many joining in the chase.

The gunman then ran into an hotel, mounted the stairs to a top room, which was fortunately unoccupied, forced a skylight, and pulled himself on to the flat roof. He was seen by scores running along a twenty foot high ledge connecting two buildings, constantly dodging in and out of sight.

In the meantime several people telephoned Scotland Yard, and soon nearly 100 police-officers threw a cordon round the area. There was an officer stationed every few yards blocking every possible exit. From the roofs above the gunman could see them, and he must have realized that his chances of escape were now practically nil.

P.C.s Rowsell and Strange had reached the roofs of other buildings nearby in their pursuit of him and P.C. Strange was the first to be shot at when he got too close. He was lucky. The bullet passed through his sleeve. A minute later the gunman fired again, this time at P.C. Rowsell. The bullet missed him, but struck some hard substance nearby, splintered, and went into the officer's eye. He staggered and called out, "He has shot me."

By this time it was realized by senior officers at the scene that the gunman was prepared to shoot it out rather than be captured, and that this was one of the rare occasions when the police should be armed. Police-Sergeant G. Lacey arrived with a pistol.

The deserter on the roof had seen that every possible way of escape had been blocked, so he darted back to the skylight, jumped through, and re-entered the room of the hotel in Cartwright Gardens. A moment later Sergeant Lacey walked into the room, pointed his pistol at him, and ordered him to put up his hands. The gunman obeyed and said, "I give in."

Detective-Superintendent Robert Higgins, then the Divisional Detective-Inspector in the West End, and the man who organized the hunt for the gunman, told him he would be charged with the murder of the young aircraftsman. He replied, "Let me think. I was there, but I didn't know I had killed anybody when I shot." Later, when charged with shooting at P.C.s Rowsell and Strange with intent to resist arrest, he replied, "What matters? I am already charged with murder."

At his trial at the Old Bailey in February 1947, prosecuting counsel said, "The evidence indicates callous indifference for the life and safety of other people, and an immediate and joyful readiness to fire a gun any time it happens to suit his personal convenience without any regard to what the results to human life and safety might be."

Sentencing the gunman to eleven years penal servitude after

he had been found not guilty of murder, but guilty of manslaughter, Mr. Justice Atkinson said, "The jury have given you the benefit of a very slender doubt, but it is plain you fired the pistol in a most reckless way, and I imagine the jury thought there was an element of bad luck in that two shots hit the airman."

P.C. Rowsell who was aged 36 at the time of this shooting, was already the holder of the British Empire Medal for Bravery shown during the blitz in Gray's Inn Road, and a Royal Humane Society Certificate for rescue from the sea while on holiday at Sheerness in 1938.

For their courage in chasing and cornering the gunman that day both he and P.C. Strange were awarded the King's Police Medal for bravery. Bertie Rowsell's left eye was so damaged by the shot that it had to be removed. When he came out of hospital he said, "I just did my job. I am lucky to be alive, and though I lost my eye I have been assured by the Home Secretary (then Mr. Chuter Ede) and the Commissioner (then Sir Harold Scott) that my job is waiting for me when I go back."

And so it was. Rowsell returned to the force, and served as a clerk under ex-Chief-Detective-Superintendent Steven Glander at Hackney until his death, following a heart attack, in September 1963.

And so ended the Bloomsbury gun battle which caused the death of a young Jamaican and permanent injury to a police constable whose career in the force was wrecked. Bertie Rowsell, 36 years old at the time he was shot, 6 ft. 3 in. tall, and 16 stone of bone and muscle, dreamed of becoming a full-time detective, and had already taken the first step as an *aide*.

From that day he was forced to spend the rest of his days in the Metropolitan police—in an office. And all because a stupid deserter-housebreaker, flushed with drink and success, thought that he was not being served quickly enough in a restaurant.

Such calamities erupting from such trifling incidents are by no means isolated. Police-officers are trained to expect the unexpected. They never know the history of a man they see about to steal a car, or the object of his theft, or whether he is armed with a deadly Browning automatic as this man was. Or as was the man, one of three seen tampering with a car in Lambeth, in August 1955.

P.C. Keith Burdett was on lone patrol in Heyford Avenue, South Lambeth, at 1 a.m. that morning of 22 August when he saw two men trying to force the door of an unattended locked car. As he ran towards them, a third man, stationed some distance from the car to keep watch for such an emergency, shouted a warning, and all three made off.

After a few yards they separated, but P.C. Burdett chased after one who ran into Old South Lambeth Road. Seconds later he heard a noise as if someone was scrambling over a wall of a bombed site into a yard which the officer knew was on the other side. He found a telephone and, still keeping the wall in sight, phoned his station for help. Within a few minutes he was joined by P.C. John Lewis, and together they went to the wall which was about 5 ft. 9 in. high.

Lewis gave Burdett a leg up, and as the officer got to the top of the wall he heard three shots fired in rapid succession, and he saw three flashes directly in front of him. He felt the blasts from the shots on the right side of his face, and at the same time felt something strike his helmet.

P.C. Burdett dropped from the wall and crouched for a moment or two. Then he and his colleague heard the man on the other side of the wall shout, "If you come over the wall I'll blow your —— head off."

Undeterred by this threat, or the danger of the gun, Burdett again prepared to mount the wall. He put his hands on the top to prise himself up, and instantly there was another shot. And two or three seconds later yet another. The officer had got his head above the top of the wall now, and he saw a man crouching about four or five feet away. He had just caught that glimpse when the second shot hit him on the index finger, and he fell backwards.

He got up again, and again looked over the wall with P.C.

Lewis, and they were in time to see the gunman skirting the wall on the far side of the yard. Just as they were debating their next move reinforcements arrived, and the area was cordoned off.

Detective-Sergeant George Frampton of the Flying Squad took charge, and he climbed over the wall with P.C. Robert Green, his driver, and P.C.s Lewis and Wyndham Morgan. Quietly and efficiently they searched the yard, and then one of them pushed at an outside lavatory door.

It did not yield, and the officer shouted to his colleagues. All four of them rushed the door and charged their shoulders against it. There was an immediate response. A hand appeared around the door and a shot was fired at them. The officers jumped back, and once again the door was slammed shut.

Sergeant Frampton shouted, "Come out." The reply was another shot fired through a ventilation hole in the door. And a voice shouted, "Come and get me, you ——." Once again the officers tried to force the door with their shoulders, but they failed.

One of them then found a heavy piece of timber, and using this as a battering ram they started bashing the door down. After a few minutes the door split, and the bottom gave way. Through this hole Sergeant Frampton saw the gunman's foot. He grabbed it, pulled, and the gun fell to the floor. All four officers piled in, and though the gunman struggled, It was hopeless.

P.C. Burdett was taken to hospital, and later the prisoner was shown the officer's helmet with the bullet indentation in it. Told he would be charged with the attempted murder of the P.C. he replied, "I shot at him to try and get away. He was a game one I'll tell you."

Then he told the police that he loaded the gun with twelve bullets because he anticipated "trouble at the Elephant," and he tried to steal the car because he wanted to get to the West End in a hurry. "I want to say that policeman had plenty of guts. I have been informed he was not seriously hurt, and I am thankful for that."

Later it emerged that the prisoner had served well in the Army, but was convicted of a civil offence, and the Army did not want him any more. That disappointed him, and he told the prison doctor that he kept hearing voices in his head telling him what to do, and usually they told him to do something wrong.

He was gaoled for seven years for wounding P.C. Burdett to resist or prevent arrest, and Mr. Justice Glyn-Jones sentencing him said, "The police-officers concerned acted with great gallantry, and ought to be commended for their conduct which was in the best tradition of the service to which they belong."

That was done, and later it was announced that P.C. Burdett had been awarded the George Medal, and Sergeant Frampton and P.C.s Lewis, Green and Morgan each with the British Empire Medal for Gallantry.

It appears that in that year, as is the case now, the police generally were the recipients of some criticism, for when presenting them with £15 cheques at Bow Street, Sir Laurence Dunne said: "It is my great pleasure to pay tribute to these gallant men. It is particularly gratifying to be able to do so now when to some extent the Metropolitan Police have been under fire. It is very proper to pay a compliment, and to express our admiration of these men, and through them to the force they represent."

Here again an attempted, and comparatively minor crime, the theft of a car, had developed into a major shooting incident. What would have happened had the three men, one armed with a loaded revolver, stolen the car and reached the West End, no one knows.

No one knows what plans had formulated in the mind of a 19-year-old Army deserter, a lad with a comparatively minor record of crime, when he secured possession of a .22 American army seven chamber revolver, and hid out in a house in Tynemouth Road, Mitcham, in March 1954. No one knows why he went absent because he had enlisted in the Army Catering Corps in December 1953, after serving a term in Borstal for shopbreaking.

Early in June the Yard received information that the deserter was in the house, and Detective-Sergeant Cyril Charles Nicholls, Detective-Constable Richard Thomas Bailey, and P.C. Arthur Holman, a dog-handler with police dog Rex III, went to the house to arrest him.

Nothing untoward happened when the officers entered the house and told the young deserter who they were. He dressed quietly, left the house quietly, and walked with them to their car. Then, as Sergeant Nicholls stooped to open the door of the car, he suddenly broke away, and darted into Thirsk Road.

Both officers and Rex III, an Alsation, gave chase, but the dog hesitated slightly when his handler fell and injured his knee. Detective Bailey, who at that time was captain of Streatham Hercules Athletic Club, and their former sprint champion, quickly overhauled the runaway, and was within a few yards of him when he turned, pointed a gun at the detective and said, "Stop, or I'll shoot you."

Then the officer saw the youth's trigger finger tighten. He heard a click as the gun was fired, and he hesitated. But there was no report. Nothing happened, and the gunman turned and ran off again. The detective drew his truncheon and threw it at his head—but missed.

As he stooped to pick it up Rex III tore past him, and was about to jump at the deserter when he turned and fired at the dog. Detective Bailey once again closed with the man to within about three or four yards and was told, "I'll kill you, you ——," and he fired again. This shot was followed by another at Rex III—and I have seen the scar left by that bullet which grazed the dog's head.

Detective Bailey was now close enough to the gunman to jump at him, and he did so. He secured a grip on the gun hand and with a quick, deft turn, threw the youth to the ground. Both were struggling violently with the gunman still gripping his gun when Sergeant Nicholls, a much older man, ran up and forced the gun away.

Neither officer hesitated to tackle and overpower this young miscreant who did not scruple to use his gun in an attempt at least to disable them, and possibly killing them. As Mr. Justice Gorman said to Detective Bailey at the Old Bailey trial, "No one having heard the case can fail to agree that your conduct on this day was worthy of the highest possible commendation. If you had turned back when this attack was made on you no one could really have blamed you."

The young deserter was found guilty of shooting at the detective with intent to murder him and was sentenced to twelve years imprisonment. Detective Bailey was awarded the George Medal, and Sergeant Nicholls the British Empire Medal for his gallantry in keeping close enough in the chase to give help and disarm the man at a crucial moment.

Sir Laurence Dunne presenting cheques to the three officers for their bravery said, "A police-officer really has only one bit of capital he can expend—his health and his life. These men did not hesitate to put both of these in jeopardy. No finer page has been written in the history of the Metropolitan Police Force."

Trivial incidents at the outset that led to grim danger which the police faced, and faced alone. Unflinching in the face of guns that spat death.

CHAPTER FOURTEEN

COURAGE AT HEIGHT

BRAVERY among officers at Scotland Yard is by no means confined to those who have to face gunmen. Practically every day of the year situations arise which test the unique courage of the policeman, who is never more appreciated than when he is needed. He is trained, and prepared, and risks his life in a variety of ways to save the public from the menace of the madman, the frenzied drunk, or the mob of drug-crazed hooligans.

He is quietly on his beat at one moment, ready at the next to dive into the Thames to save an attempted suicide; to climb dangerous heights to rescue a drunk, or to tackle the man with the knife or the cosh, whom he has good reason to suspect is wanted for some previous villainy. They come from all parts of the country, from Scotland to my own Cornwall, but their courage does not vary.

One dark winters night towards the end of 1962 a man had been looking at the wine when it was very, very red, when for some reason, known only to himself, he decided to climb to the eighteenth floor of a block of flats under construction at Camberwell. He was so drunk that he hoisted himself on to a crane tower just above a twelve-inch girder, nearly 200 feet from the ground. Apparently no one saw him climb, but a few minutes later passersby in the road below, were made aware of his presence above. He started throwing planks, and any other missile he could find, at them.

These citizens looked up, and in the pale moonlight, could just make out a figure swaying perilously on the crane tower.

Some phoned the fire brigade, others phoned the police. Everyone wondered why anyone should want to make such a perilous climb at midnight—a climb the gentleman concerned would almost certainly not have dared in daylight—and sober.

Within a few moments fire bells clanged and a fire engine arrived. The officers looked up, then shone a searchlight on the lone figure dicing with death. Seconds later came P.C. Richard Thomas, aged 38, a former miner from Bridgend in Wales, and at that time, officially a dog-handler. Close behind him came another dog-handler, P.C. Norman Bartholomew, aged 41, formerly of Edinburgh.

P.C. Thomas took one look and immediately started to climb the partly built stairway to the 18th floor. Closely behind him came P.C. Bartholomew. They reached the top and then gently edged their way along the twelve-inch girder towards the drunken man. Soon, Thomas, who was still leading, got to within three feet of the man who was still swaying madly in the breeze in desperate danger of falling.

Then suddenly he appeared to lose his grip, and he fell. He was falling to certain death when, as quick as a flash, P.C. Thomas reached out and grabbed him by his raincoat. For an instant both were in peril, then P.C. Bartholomew acted with equal ability. He leaned forward, grabbed P.C. Thomas round the waist, and held grimly on.

Nightmare seconds followed. Firemen and an anxious crowd watched in the glare of the searchlight. For a moment it looked as if all three might come thundering down the 165 feet to the ground. But the officers, both powerful men, held on. P.C. Bartholomew was sitting astride the girder and he locked his legs around it.

Then P.C. Thomas got a better grip on the man and gradually and, thanks to the strength of his powerful arms, hauled him to the girder. Then both officers carried him down to a waiting ambulance. Both men had risked their lives for a drunk. A Welshman and a Scot—but good, honest, durable, dependable cops.

On 14 December of that year Sir Robert Blundell, the Chief

Metropolitan Magistrate, presented to both £20 cheques from the Reward Fund for their bravery, and he said, "As he (the drunk) was passing P.C. Thomas grabbed at the man with his hand, and held him swinging by his raincoat in mid-air. It should be appreciated that had not P.C. Thomas grabbed the man as he fell past he would have fallen to the ground, and had not P.C. Bartholomew been able to hold on to his colleague it must have resulted in death both to the man and P.C. Thomas."

Later both officers were awarded the British Empire Medal. One hopes that the man whose life they saved will not be included among the numbers who so consequently grumble about the activities of the police who are only doing their duty in enforcing traffic and other regulations.

It doesn't matter whether the man is drunk or mentally deranged, the Yard men will do their duty, despite the danger. Only, later, when the ordeal is over, do the majority of them fully appreciate the risk they ran, and think of their wives and families.

In instances of dealing with the mentally deranged the trained officer, although open to attack, rarely, if ever, draws his truncheon. He pleads, he coaxes, and defends himself as best he can, while getting ever nearer to the person concerned. No effort is spared to prevent injury to the man, who for some reason, is not responsible for his actions.

An outstanding example of this happened at a Rehabilita tion Centre in High Street, Elstree, which exists for the re-settlement of men who have been mentally ill. In March 1963, one of the men under instruction there at that time, a man of 23, became suspected of a number of minor thefts in the Centre. Then came two fires which he was believed to have caused. There was insufficient evidence for any police action to be taken, but in the circumstances, he was asked to leave by 3.30 p.m. on Monday, 25 March.

He appeared to accept this notice with good grace. He had lunch at the Centre and at 2.15 p.m. was seen walking along the street outside the Centre carrying an axe. Five minutes later he was seen on the north wing roof brandishing the axe and threatening to throw it at an official who tried to approach him.

The warden telephoned Elstree police and within a few minutes two officers arrived. They shouted to the man and tried to get him down, but he immediately started to throw tiles, slates, coping stones and pieces of wood he was chopping from the roof, at them.

Further police assistance was summoned, and at about 3.10 p.m. Station-Sergeant Leslie John Mackey, aged 38, and Detective-Constable Frank Victor Keylock, aged 32, arrived, the latter with a large safety shield which the police keep for such emergencies.

These two officers immediately volunteered to go on to the roof, which varied from thirty to fifty feet from ground level, and try to get the axe-wielding man down. As there was only one safety shield Sergeant Mackey gave that to Detective Keylock. Then he looked around for protection for himself and decided on a pig-bin lid.

They had learned that the man had earlier taken an overdose of sleeping tablets, and knew that his removal from the roof was a matter of urgency. Meanwhile the man himself was busily tearing tiles from the roof and throwing them at anyone who came within range. He was originally wearing a coat and woollen pullover, but he discarded these items of clothing, and remained in just a shirt and trousers.

Mackey and Keylock climbed out of a top window, and started clambering up the sloping tiles towards the man. To reach him they had to negotiate several parts of angled roof, and all the time they were showered with missiles which they either dodged, or warded off with their shields. To make matters worse there was a very strong wind blowing, catching their shields, and making progress extremely hazardous.

Sergeant Mackey kept talking to the man. He would talk for a few minutes, advance a few steps, then talk again. But every time he advanced the man retreated. Several times he disappeared from the view of the officers, collected more missiles to throw at them, shouting all the time, "If you come near me I'll chop your bloody heads off," or once when Sergeant Mackey got too close, "You'll get this axe between your eyes if you aren't careful."

The roof was steep, and neither officer could be sure of a firm foot or handhold, but they persevered, and eventually got to within a few feet of the man who then aimed vicious blows at them with his axe. Mackey and Keylock warded off these blows with the safety shield and the pig-bin lid which they held in front of them.

Then, just as they got to close quarters and attempted to grab the man Detective Keylock slipped, and lost his grip on the safety shield. The man immediately aimed a blow at him with the axe, but Sergeant Mackey dived across in front of his helpless colleague, and caught the axe blow with his pig-bin lid. This gave the detective time to recover his shield.

By this time other officers from Elstree had arrived on the roof and were following close in the wake of Sergeant Mackey. Now and then one or two of these had to lie flat on the roof to dodge the constant barrage of missiles. The sight of police uniforms appeared to enrage the man even further, and he was in constant danger of falling.

At odd points there was no parapet on the sloping slate roof; nothing but the rainwater guttering below the roof edge to stop anyone sliding off and falling forty to fifty feet on to the hard surface below. It was at one such point that Keylock and Mackey got close enough to come to grips. All three fell to the roof, but the two officers clung on and the axe slid off the roof. The man still struggled violently, but other officers arrived, and he was firmly held.

To prevent the man struggling further Sergeant Mackey tied his hands together with his tie. He then tied a rope which had been supplied by firemen round the man's body, looped it round a nearby chimney stack, and preceded him down a fire brigade escape ladder. Then the man was removed to hospital for emergency treatment.

The axe this man wielded was fourteen inches long and

F

weighed about seven pounds. The force with which he used it punctured the pig-bin lid in four places. One officer who was on the roof with them said later, "I followed them on to the roof and had a close view of his attacks on them and feel that they both displayed great courage and disregard of their personal safety. They made no effort to draw their truncheons, but concentrated solely on warding off the missiles and the axe and trying to pacify the man."

Both Sergeant Mackey and Detective Keylock were commended by the Commissioner and on 23 April, it was announced that they had been awarded British Empire Medals for bravery. On that same day a similar award was announced to a Special-Constable for his courage in the rescue of a boy who had absconded from a mental home.

On the night of 3 October 1962, this boy, aged 13, climbed 150 feet to the top of the Kennington gasholder, familiar to everyone who watches cricket. And there he clung in terror, frightened to move, and his shouts for help unheard in the biting, whistling wind.

After a while he was spotted by a valves man, who after summoning the police and fire brigade, climbed a cat ladder to within a few feet of the boy who by now was hanging by one arm from the girder with his feet on one of the supporting struts. His other hand gripped a rope hanging from a flagpole, and the valve man could not reach him.

Everyone watching in petrified silence wondered how long the boy could hold on. How long it would be before he fell to certain death. Then along came Special-Constable John Laurence, aged 30. He was off-duty at the time, but he acted without hesitation. He left the van he was driving and climbed to the very roof of the holder.

Once there he walked along until he was immediately above the boy where there happened to be a revolving wheel jutting out between the side of the holder and the girders. Laurence tied a rope around himself, leant over, and was just able to reach the boy's arms which he grasped.

And there he hung on. By this time the boy was crying, and

screaming in terror. He was swaying in the wind, but Laurence held grimly on until, after a few minutes, the boy became unconscious.

Laurence then began to realize that if help did not arrive soon he would be forced to let go. Below him he could see the lights, and the safety of the ground—and the firemen working to reach him. Every muscle screamed in agony, but the plucky man held on until the firemen arrived, rigged up a bosun's chair, and he was able, thankfully, to pass the rope round the boy's body and watch him lowered to safety.

Few people are privileged to witness these acts of heroism, but there was at least one outstanding exception. Millions of viewers must have seen the television recording of the courage of a young policewoman who, when standing on a rooftop edge sixty feet above the ground, snatched a baby from the arms of a man threatening to jump.

Policewoman Margaret Cleland, aged 23, stationed at Grays Inn Road police station, had been summoned to the rooftop high above Coram Street, Bloomsbury, on 3 March 1964, when previous attempts to capture the man and his 22-month-old son had failed, and someone hit upon the idea, "This is a job for a woman."

W.P.C. Cleland, $3\frac{1}{2}$ years in the force, arrived on the roof to see the man with the baby firmly held in his arms, sitting with his legs through the roof edge iron balustrade. Below a circle of volunteers stretched out a safety net, but firemen who had also been called, had to lower an extension ladder when the man showed an increased intention of jumping.

Woman Police-Constable Cleland, who says she has no head for heights, edged her way along a foot-wide gulley at the edge of the roof, but when she got to within about six feet of the man he told her that if she came any nearer he would jump. There was a bitter wind blowing, and soon the young officer was numb with cold—but she kept the man talking.

She began talking about little things; anything that came to her mind, and which she thought might attract and keep a man's attention. Then she learned that he came originally from a place near her home in Dumbartonshire, and they talked about Scotland. They talked for an hour and a quarter, and all that time a tense and hushed crowd below watched and waited. Television and Press cameras were focussed on the two vital figures in this human drama.

Then the baby began to cry, and W.P.C. Cleland told the father that the child was suffering from the cold. She had seen some baby's clothes at his feet, and she picked up a little coat and asked if she could put it on.

The man hesitated. Earlier he had said he trusted no one. Then Miss Cleland called the baby by name, and it turned its head. She walked quietly forward with the coat in her hand as if to put it over the child then, quick as lightning, she grabbed.

She grabbed the baby with her right hand and the man with her left. She kept pulling with all her might fearful in case the parapet gave way. Then she fell backwards, and to the relief of all, the baby came with her. Two ambulance men, acting with commendable promptitude, immediately jumped forward and held the man.

The crowd below sighed with relief, and when a few minutes later W.P.C. Cleland emerged from the house they gave her a tremendous cheer and clapped her all the way to the police car. One woman rushed up to her with her arms outstretched and wanted to kiss her. "And do you know," said Miss Cleland later, "I felt so relieved I wanted to kiss her back."

That night the dramatic scene was shown on Television, and next day flowers and congratulations poured into Grays Inn Road police station for the courageous young woman who came to London and joined the Metropolitan Police Force "for adventure."

Later, Sir Joseph Simpson, the Metropolitan Police Commissioner, gave her an official commendation for "outstanding courage," and on 11 May, when she was handed a cheque for £20 from the Bow Street Police Reward Fund, Mr. K. J. P. Barraclough, the magistrate, described her as "A very brave young woman." On 18 August 1964, the *London Gazette* announced that the Queen had awarded her the George Medal for bravery.

Such instances indicate the preparedness of our police, and their ability, courage and initiative in dealing with any situation. In any crash of any kind, road, rail or air, they are almost invariably among the first on the scene, anxious to help and, if possible, save lives.

At 11.28 p.m. on 2 December 1955, an accident occurred about two hundred yards east of Barnes railway station when an electric passenger train from Waterloo ran into the back of a goods train. The first coach of the passenger train was derailed, and the wreckage from the front part of this coach and the rear of the goods train was jammed beneath the supports of the Queens Ride Bridge over the railway, and caught fire because of short circuiting with the live rail.

Within moments there was a fierce fire, and messages were flashed to Scotland Yard for assistance. Police-Sergeant Norman George Loxley, aged 30, and P.C. Thomas Oliver, aged 40, were on duty in a patrol car with P.C. Ronald Croft, when they received the message, and they reached Barnes railway station at 11.37 p.m. Running on to the platform they saw the fire whereupon Sergeant Loxley ordered P.C. Croft to return to the car and signal for the fire brigade and ambulances to be sent.

Sergeant Loxley and P.C. Oliver then jumped on to the track, ignoring a warning about the live rail, and ran to the blazing train. When they got near the sergeant handed a first aid box, which he had brought from the car, to a young woman who said she was a nurse, and was attending a seriously injured man.

Both officers then saw a man's feet protruding from underneath a pile of burning wreckage, about a yard from the conductor rail. And they saw that the feet were moving. The heat was so intense that Sergeant Loxley had to take off his raincoat and hold it in front of him as a shield to get near.

P.C. Oliver grasped a blazing carriage seat which was lying across the man's body and levered it up while the sergeant grabbed the man's ankles and tried to pull him clear, but they failed; and the burning heat, already singeing their hair, forced them back momentarily.

Sergeant Loxley tried again, but he swallowed some smoke and hot air and fell backwards. P.C. Oliver then put his serge jacket over his head, and going in again, managed to dislodge the burning seat and other debris. Then, with the help of Sergeant Loxley, and others who had now arrived, they pulled the man clear.

The man was a locomotive driver going home from duty, and although very severely burned his life was saved. P.C. Oliver saw another man behind him but the heat was too intense for the officers to do anything further. As it was they both received such burns and abrasions that they were on the sick list for five days.

Thirteen people lost their lives in that crash, and at the public inquiry which followed Colonel G. R. S. Wilson, who presided, said to Loxley and Oliver, "It is undoubtedly due to you that this man is still alive. It was a very fine piece of work."

And in October 1956 it was announced that both officers had been awarded the George Medal. They were decorated by the Queen who said, "Well done." Before that, however, each received cheques for £15 from Sir Laurence Dunne, then the Chief Magistrate, who said, "This is an excellent example of the way in which the Metropolitan Police carry out their duties in every sort of emergency. They do not hesitate to hazard their health and lives in safeguarding the property and lives of others."

CHAPTER FIFTEEN

WAR AND THE SERGEANT

I T is the ability of police-officers to cope with any situation, no matter how unusual or how difficult or dangerous, that arouses admiration for them, particularly among those who have been fortunate, or unfortunate, enough to have been involved in any incident demanding their attention.

Not only is it when they are faced with guns, or knives, or desperate cosh-swinging criminals that they have earned honour for themselves and for the force. It has happened in a variety of ways—in fires, in saving people from drowning, and even in the stopping of frightened runaway horses. Because they are on patrol they are often first on the scene of a fire, and it is then they have to use their initiative, and call upon their courage, to carry out frequently dangerous rescue operations before the arrival of the fire brigade.

Metropolitan Police-officers have shown equally conspicuous gallantry *under* fire. During World War II more than 3,000 officers were released from the force for service with the Royal Navy, the Army, and the Royal Air Force, and no fewer than 192 regular policemen, and 18 members of the Civil Staff lost their lives on active service. Most of these were serving with the R.A.F. because at one period the only form of armed service for which they were allowed to volunteer was as pilots or observers in the R.A.F. or Fleet Air Arm. Of the 1,696 who joined that service, mainly in Bomber Command, 383 lost their lives.

More than 200 police-officers returned, with British, Dutch, French and American decorations for gallantry. They included police-constables who became Squadron Leaders, and sergeants who became Captains and Majors.

At home during those war years there was no truce with the criminals. And the uniformed men and detectives carried on the battle against crime, under the constant danger of whistling bombs, incendiary bombs, and the V.1's and the V.2's from day and night German raiders. For forty-seven of the sixty-eight months that the war lasted London was under more or less intensive attack from the air, with the police force in the front line of defence.

It was on 7 September 1940, that the enemy started his blitz in earnest, and by constant night bombing tried his utmost to disorganize London, and break the spirit of its people. That he failed is due in no small measure to the leadership and example set by the police who, as Sir Winston Churchill said in a broadcast in 1942, "Have been in it everywhere all the time."

It was during this big blitz that stories of the outstanding courage of Police-Sergeant James Arthur Robson began to emerge. It seemed that in almost every other major incident in the W.C.1. area of London where homes or offices had been hit, and people trapped, the sergeant was there leading rescue squads, and calming and helping the injured.

Sergeant Robson joined the Metropolitan Police Force in 1928 from his home at Talkin, a village near Carlisle, in Cumberland. As a teenager he had had two ambitions, firstly to become a policeman, and secondly to swim the three-quarters of a mile wide lake beside his home.

But when he came to London, and was stationed at Kings Cross Road, this rather slim, rather shy young man, still was unable to swim. His ability as a wrestler and boxer soon became apparent, and in his spare time he taught himself to swim in adjacent baths. And on one of his early annual leaves he swam across that lake.

After eight years on the beat he was promoted to sergeant, and in 1936 was transferred to Grays Inn Road police station. Here he spent many of his off-duty hours in helping to organize and run youth clubs, and training youngsters in Judo, wrestling, boxing and swimming. More than one of these youths were so impressed with the sergeant's leadership that they later joined the police force.

Sergeant Robson was that sort of man. A born leader, a strict disciplinarian, but only too willing and anxious to help anyone in trouble. When the bombing started in earnest he was on constant patrol in charge of a number of junior officers. Their unenviable task was to pinpoint where the bombs fell then rush there with the object of helping the injured or freeing anyone trapped in buildings which had been hit.

During the really "Big Blitz" in 1941 the area for which he was responsible was subjected to a most severe bombardment, and one night when the sergeant a married man, was off-duty, scores of incendiaries started a big fire in a building in Queen's Square, Holborn. He could see the blaze from his bedroom window, and decided he would go out and give what help he could.

When he got to the blazing building he first established that no one was inside, but it quickly became apparent that the fire fighters could not control the flames, and the building, in danger of collapsing, was threatening to trap more than one hundred people, men, women and children, sheltering in a nearby air raid shelter.

It was decided that these people, despite the danger of the bombardment which was still in progress, must be moved and Sergeant Robson took charge of this task. He entered the shelter, calmed the frightened people, and then quietly and efficiently shepherded them from the danger zone to another place of comparative safety.

It was this action, carried out when he was off-duty, which culminated in his being summoned to Buckingham Palace and being decorated by the late King George VI with the British Empire Medal, and the citation recalling his outstanding gallantry and devotion to duty added:

"On all occasions he has, by his leadership and courage, been an example and an inspiration to all with whom he came into contact. He has rescued a number of trapped persons from bombed buildings, and on one occasion, although he was not on duty, he made strenuous efforts to check a fire. It became necessary, however, to evacuate a large air raid shelter nearby, and in spite of the heavy bombardment in progress, he carried out this work with complete absence of panic among the shelterers."

Sergeant Robson continued with the good work. He was always at Action Stations, leading the rescuers, and soothing the frightened. Night after night his slight figure was a symbol of strength and encouragement as he dived amid blazing rafters ensuring at every one of hundreds of incidents he attended that no one was left trapped and helpless.

His fearlessness, even when bombs were falling all around, astounded even his colleagues in the force. At times bombs fell so close that they had to throw themselves into gutters to escape the blast, but the sergeant, "Robbie" to them, was never ruffled. He led them on, and they wished for no other leader.

No one knows the number of bombing incidents he attended nor the total number of people he dug from demolished homes, but it was late in 1943 when Hitler was indulging in tip-and-run raids on London, that Sergeant Robson's supreme efforts in rescuing a man and a woman trapped deep in the wreckage of four houses in Birkenhead Street, Kings Cross, led to his second summons to Buckingham Palace. And on this occasion King George VI pinned the George Medal to his tunic.

It was round about midnight that the bomb smacked into the houses, exploded with a giant roar, and felled them into a solid mass of smouldering rubble. Within a few minutes Sergeant Robson was on the spot with P.C.s Stanley Evans and Stanley Foxton. They had heard the bomb falling, and had seen the bricks and wood flung into the air as it detonated.

They stood beside the rubble and listened. There, after a few seconds, they heard faint cries. There were two separate cries for help. It quickly became evident that a man and a woman were trapped beneath the great mass of bricks, and that both were somewhere in the middle. Led by their sergeant the officers commenced rescue operations.

Starting by way of a basement entrance that had been left partially clear they began tunnelling through. Inch by inch they burrowed their way into the shifting bricks and timber, shoring them up as they went, and passing the debris back to one another. And every few minutes they shouted encouragement to the trapped man and woman, telling them, "We are on our way."

They dug at the bricks with their bare hands, passing them back to one another. It had to be a narrow tunnel, just wide enough to hold one man, and they took it in turns to lead the way, with the sergeant supervising the shoring of the constantly shifting rubble. Hour after hour they dug their way in until they were out of sight of other rescue workers who had arrived.

Night gave way to day, and still the three men toiled. Then came another problem. When they were ten feet or so inside the tunnel the atmosphere became so foul that they could not breathe. Oxygen was sent for, and pumped into the tunnel to enable them to carry on.

Then, in the early hours of the morning, they reached the man. They cleared the debris from him and hauled him safely through their makeshift tunnel. Outside doctors attended to him, and he was taken to hospital. In the distance, however, they could still hear the cries of the woman who they learned, had lived next door to the man.

Sergeant Robson and the two police-constables went back, and headed their tunnel in the direction of her cries. Hour after hour they carried on with their back-breaking task, and neither of these three brave men in constant danger under tons of shifting debris, and working only by the light of their torches, sought or called for any relief.

After another two hours, and when their tunnel measured over fifteen feet from the basement door entrance, Sergeant Robson reached the trapped woman. She had been in bed on the ground floor with her baby daughter when the bomb fell. They were both covered in debris, and the woman could not move.

Carefully and gently the officers started clearing away the

bricks and timber that covered the woman. Then came two ghastly shocks. They found that the baby was dead, and the woman was trapped by both legs by heavy metal bars which could not be shifted by hand. Sergeant Robson explained the position to other rescue workers outside, and they sent for oxy-acetylene burners.

While this was being done the sergeant went back through the tunnel to comfort the woman until its arrival. They sat there together, alone in the darkness, breathing the foul air, the frightened, injured woman, and the dust-smothered policeman. After a while she complained of the pain in her legs, so Sergeant Robson crawled through the tunnel again, and returned with morphia which he injected to ease her pain.

At frequent intervals, far too frequent intervals, the rubble shifted, and timbers cracked ominously. Only the sergeant realized how ominously, for only he knew how precarious was the temporary cave he had made under the mountain of rubble. At last the oxy-acetylene apparatus arrived, and the sergeant still sat with the woman as the metal which trapped her legs was burned through and she was freed.

Slowly and gently he supervised her removal through the tunnel. He had lost all count of time. His only thought was that this woman he had never seen before was in trouble and needed help. But from the time he had started digging towards her until the moment he assisted her into an ambulance outside practically thirteen hours had elapsed.

And when Sergeant Robson went to Buckingham Palace to receive the George Medal, he took with him P.C.s Evans and Foxton, his two lieutenants who showed equal fearlessness and determination to rescue the trapped man and woman. Both these officers, who later joined the Royal Navy, were awarded the British Empire Medal.

The citation announcing their awards drew attention to the fact that the three officers had ignored, in addition to all other hazards, the danger of a party wall which was hanging at a most precarious angle above them all the time they were working.

Of Sergeant Robson it said, "Without his skill at tunnelling it would have been impossible to get to the woman in time to save her life." And of the three officers it added, "They showed great courage and devotion to duty in very dangerous and difficult circumstances."

In between these examples of heroism and self-sacrifice Sergeant Robson, of course, continued with normal police duties, and at one time supervised a number of *aides* to C.I.D.—budding detectives—in catching burglars, and housebreakers, and looters. Like so many of his colleagues he was never really off-duty. He took great pride in his job, in his men, and in the wardens and rescue workers who so often came to his aid.

The last bomb to fall in the Metropolitan Police district was at Waltham Abbey in March 1945, and the nightly horrors faced by Sergeant Robson and so many like him, ended. Gradually the Metropolitan Policemen returned to more normal duties, but the story of heroism on the part of "Robbie" was by no means concluded.

In the summer of 1949 he was on annual leave at Kingsgate, near Broadstairs, and about to enjoy, as a powerful and accomplished swimmer, his daily dip when he heard people on the beach shouting, "Help, she's drowning." Sergeant Robson at that moment was doing what he so often did—helping someone else. He was assisting an old lady in pushing a perambulator over rough sand.

He looked up on hearing the cries for help and saw out at sea, about 200 yards from the beach, a young girl obviously in grave difficulties. There was a heavy sea running at the time, and accompanying it was a dangerous undertow. In fact a little further along the coast red flags had been hoisted warning that there should be no swimming.

Sergeant Robson was already wearing swimming trunks under his suit, so he dropped the pram, slipped off his clothes, bolted down the beach, and within a minute was fighting his way through the waves, and a terrible mass of seaweed, towards the girl.

As he swam he saw one man had waded into the sea up to

his neck—but that man could not swim. About one hundred yards out he passed another man swimming towards the girl, but it was obvious that this man was just about all in. And as the sergeant passed him he turned and headed back towards the beach.

When the sergeant reached the girl she was unconscious. He took hold of her, turned on his back, placed the girl across his chest, and, using the back stroke headed for the beach. Time and again great masses of seaweed tangled themselves around his legs, and he had to kick with all his strength to free them. On shore anxious parents and holidaymakers watched anxiously as again and again they saw his progress halted.

After what seemed an age Sergeant Robson landed, and handed the unconscious girl to people ready and waiting to give her artificial respiration. As they took her the Sergeant lay on the beach, completely exhausted. Only his terrific will-power, and his superb fitness had enabled him to save the child. No other man on that beach that day was capable of doing it.

Then quietly, without fuss, and as soon as he saw that the child had recovered, the sergeant collected his clothes and slipped away. No one, as far as he knew, realized who he was, or knew where he was staying. He preferred it that way. Like so many heroes he was somewhat shy.

That same evening there was a knock on the door of his "digs," and on answering it Sergeant Robson saw a man and his wife. The conversation went something like this.

Man: I believe—no, now I have seen you, I know; you are the man who saved the life of our daughter this afternoon.

Sergeant Robson: Well, I did bring a little girl ashore. Is she all right?

Man: Yes, she is all right now, and my wife and I want to tell you how much we are indebted to you. Without your courage we should not have had our daughter now. We cannot thank you, or praise you enough.

Sergeant Robson: I am glad I was there, and I am happy that she is well again.

Man: Where do you come from? London?

Sergeant Robson: Yes, I am a Metropolitan Police-Officer.
Man: Well I never. So am I!

By a curious quirk of fate Sergeant Robson had saved the life of the daughter of a fellow officer; Diane, the ten-year-old daughter of Detective-Sergeant Frank Cooper of Scotland Yard's Flying Squad, who was also on annual leave at Kingsgate with his family. And they had never met before.

What was said between these two brother officers then is not on record; neither has it ever been revealed how Detective-Sergeant Cooper traced the man who had saved his daughter, but you can trust a Flying Squad man to do that.

This further heroic effort on the part of Sergeant Robson reached the ears of authority and in February 1950, he was ordered to Cannon Row police station where he was awarded the Royal Humane Society's Bronze Life-Saving Medal.

Many of his colleagues who were there to honour him heard him make this reply to speeches praising his heroism: "The greatest pleasure I get out of life is giving a helping hand to others." And everyone who had served with him throughout the years knew just how true that was.

Unfortunately, but due no doubt to the strenuous life he had lived, Sergeant Robson had to retire from the force because of ill-health in January 1960. In 31 years of faithful and heroic service, and in addition to the Awards of the British Empire Medal, the George Medal and Life-Saving Bronze, Medal, he collected no fewer than eighteen commendations for acts ranging from stopping runaway horses to arresting armed mailbag robbers.

CHAPTER SIXTEEN

FACING A BOMB

WITH the grim shadow of war hanging ominously, the people of this country faced another determined enemy early in 1939 —the Irish Republican Army. Members had quietly infiltrated into London and the provinces, found themselves lodgings, and started making their crude, but highly dangerous, home-made bombs.

Between 16 January and 18 May of that year they had committed more than 100 outrages. Life and property were in danger. No one knew where they would strike next or when a bomb might be thrown through their window or placed in their letter box.

Practically every Scotland Yard officer, and certainly every Special Branch man, worked overtime during those months to capture and convict these terrorists, who swore to continue with their illegal and illogical practises "until Britain withdraws her troops from Ireland."

Typical of their most dangerous exploits was that in March. Four I.R.A. men hired a car in Hammersmith to take them, they said, to Ewell. On the way there they overpowered a chauffeur, and while one drove the car back to Hammersmith the others prepared the time fuses on bombs which they had secreted in their suitcases.

They stopped on Hammersmith Bridge, and placed one suit-case on each side before making off. A minute or so later a man walking over the bridge saw one of the suitcases and opened it. He saw a mass of burning rags and heard a hissing noise, so he tossed the case into the river.

He walked on a few yards, and then heard a terrific explosion. He looked back and saw a column of water rise from the Thames where he had thrown the case. It reached a height of sixty feet. Seconds later came a second explosion from the other side of the bridge. This, caused by a bomb in the second suit-case, caused damage which cost £1,000 before the bridge could be made fit for use again.

No one had any doubts as to the fatality that these bombs could cause, and they were planted all over London, Birming-ham and Manchester. One man was killed in Manchester and scores of people were injured. By the end of March nearly forty culprits had been convicted and sentenced to terms of penal servitude varying from five to twenty years.

Still the outrages continued, and Scotland Yard detectives were literally run off their feet in dealing with scores of such incidents, and, at the same time, trying to cope with the normal outbreak of robberies and other crimes. Vice, too, was pretty rampant in the West End at that time, and a special Vice Squad had been formed to halt, or at least, curb it.

Among the officers appointed to this Squad, which had its headquarters at Vine Street, the station which preceded West End Central, was the then Detective-Inspector Robert Fabian; later to win international fame as "Fabian of the Yard." Fabian had joined the Metropolitan Police as a police-constable, but he had unrivalled knowledge of the West End clubs and the men, and the rackets, behind them.

On the evening of 24 June that year he was sitting in his office at Vine Street typing a report on inquiries he had been making that day, when there came a terrific explosion which rattled the window, and shook the doors of that old station.

It came from the direction of Piccadilly Circus, and as Fab-ian made for his gas mask, with which the police had already been issued, a gust of hot air blew across the room. Fabian grabbed his hat and mask and ran towards the Circus.

When he arrived it was already jammed with people. Two or three uniformed officers were already there keeping back a curious crowd from the corner of Glasshouse Street where it was evident the explosion had taken place. The pavement was littered with broken glass and cigarette and cigar boxes from one shop, and lingerie from the next. The force of the explosion had blown out nearly all the lights of the Circus.

Fabian forced his way through the crowd of sightseers, and, when he surveyed the wreckage, surmised immediately that the damage had been caused by another I.R.A. bomb. He stood quietly for a moment and "Gave his eyes a treat" as he would say. His eyes rapidly examined the wreckage on the pavement searching for any clue, anything that might indicate exactly where the bomb had been placed, or any part of it which might have been left and which could bear a fingerprint.

Suddenly he spotted a brown paper parcel, partially hidden from his view behind a traffic signpost. It looked undamaged. That was curious, he thought, and he walked over to it to have a closer look. As he bent to examine it he saw that it had been carefully wrapped, and that the ends of the paper had been fastened with strips of adhesive tape.

It was not the sort of wrapping one would expect in a purchase from a West End shop, and the detective's suspicions were aroused. He gently touched the parcel with the tips of his fingers. It was hot! Far, far too hot for any normal package.

Fabian, fully aware of the activities of the I.R.A., turned and shouted to his colleagues, "Keep the crowd back further. I think this is another bomb." Gingerly he picked up the parcel and looked around for a bucket of water in which to dump it. There was none in sight.

There he stood, feeling very much alone, holding a parcel which seemed to be getting hotter every second, and which he feared might explode at any moment, and blow him, if not others, to pieces. All around him lay the debris of the bomb which had exploded. There was no doubting the deadliness of the weapon he held.

His knowledge of explosives at that time was next to negligible, but he knew that something had to be done, and done quickly. By this time several hundred people had gathered round the Circus. Many of them guessed what was in the parcel, and they watched in silence, gazing at the lone figure, wondering what he was going to do.

Round about this time the fire brigade arrived and here, thought Fabian, was his safety valve. Here was water. Plenty of it. He approached a fire brigade officer and asked for a bucket of water. They had no bucket. "What do you think we represent? Southend?" jocularly replied the officer. And both laughed.

Fabian returned alone to the parcel bomb, and decided there was only one thing to do. Dismantle it. He knelt on the pavement, placed the parcel carefully in front of him, and pulled out his old, and rather blunt, pocket knife. He cut the adhesive tape, then carefully and slowly unfolded the paper at one end. He worked his hand gently inside, and felt something soft wrapped in greaseproof paper.

Inch-by-inch he eased it out. It was a stick of gelignite! Yellow, softish gelignite with its sickly smell. Fabian placed it gingerly beside him, and felt inside the parcel again. Seven times he did this, each time pulling out a four ounce stick of Polar Ammon gelignite.

The crowd, now standing at a safe distance, and kept back by Fabian's colleagues, watched in fascinated silence. Some who watched could bear the strain no longer. They understood the danger, appreciated the terrible sight an explosion would cause, and turned away. Others were seen offering a silent prayer for the lone, brave officer.

When he had extracted seven sticks Fabian coolly separated them, placing each at some distance from the other, so that if one exploded the others would not be affected by the detonation. He returned to the parcel, knelt again, and found an eighth stick and the vital part he had been anxiously seeking, the fuse. Unaware at that time that the grating of the blade of his blunt knife could explode the gelignite he sliced this stick and removed the fuse which he placed in his pocket.

Still working quietly and with gentle skill he extracted two more sticks of gelignite—making a total of forty ounces. Then he got down on all fours and peered inside the contraption.

He saw a small pile of grey powder in the centre of which was a green rubber balloon. As he pulled this out his hands burned and blistered with the acid—but he knew then that he had won. He had dismantled the deadly bomb before the acid had had time to eat through the balloon to the explosive.

Still without a bucket Fabian calmly slashed all of the sticks of gelignite into small pieces, placed them separately into cigar and cigarette boxes which had been blown out by the explosion, and, with the aid of several colleagues, carried the lot into Vine Street police station where they were dumped into a well-filled row of red buckets which lined the hall.

Few of the thousands who know Bob Fabian, including many of his colleagues in the Fleet Street area where he now works, knew of this act of heroism, or are aware that for his courage that night he was awarded the King's Police Medal for Gallantry. He never talks about it. It was another job. Somebody had to do something about the bomb, and he was the senior officer on the spot.

Some days before he was summoned to Buckingham Palace Fabian received word that he was expected at a certain public house in the City. Nobody knew what it was about or who wanted him. The message he received was that he ought to go, and thinking possibly, it was an informant who wanted to give him information on a crime, Fabian went.

When he pushed open the doors of the Saloon bar he was startled to see the biggest collection of thieves and rogues of all descriptions he had ever seen assembled under the same roof. And two rushed forward, one with a cigar, the other with a large whisky which they thrust into his hands. He wondered what it was all about. Some of these men he himself had been responsible for sending to prison.

They apologized for the mystery call, said their spokesman, a well-known gang leader, but they had heard about the bomb he had dismantled, and they had a present for him. It was a large bronze medal, about the same size as the King's Medal, and on it was engraved the words—"To Robert Fabian for Heroism—from the boys."

In normal circumstances Fabian was their enemy, but crooks, excepting the vicious and the gunmen, have a peculiar code of their own, and they respected the officer and his courage. This was their way of showing it, despite the fact that they realized for certainty that on the morrow, if he had any evidence against them, he would not hesitate in arresting any one of them.

On 6 February 1940, King George VI presented Fabian with the real medal and said to him, "I am pleased to make your acquaintance and congratulate you on your gallantry." And the official citation said, "At great risk he threw himself upon an I.R.A. bomb in Piccadilly Circus, disconnected it, and prevented a possible serious loss of life."

Quite a number of people in other parts of London were injured in half a dozen or so explosions that warm June night, and Special Branch officers joined with divisional detectives and worked all night tracking down the young Irish extremists responsible.

During the course of these outrages Scotland Yard itself was threatened. Undercover officers learned that the I.R.A. planned to ride a tricycle loaded with explosives into the courtyard and leave it there set with a time-bomb. Both big gates which gave entrance from the Embankment at one side, and Whitehall on the other, were closed and guarded for some time.

Women officers in plain clothes and scores of detectives kept watch day and night on many suspects, and scores were rounded up and imprisoned. In several instances young extremists were armed but the Yard men never carried arms.

Not one of the hundreds of officers I know at the Yard is in favour of carrying a gun. They believe that this would result in gun battles, and in more and more criminals arming themselves, and shooting it out with the police in old Chicago fashion.

Fabian never carried a gun during his inquiry into the murder of Alec de Antiques, a modest little greengrocer, father of six, who was shot down in Charlotte Street on 27 April 1947, by gunmen who tried to hold up and rob a jeweller's shop. His life and that of his colleagues, Detective-Superintendent Robert Higgins and Chief-Inspector (later Superintendent) Fred Hodge were threatened several times during the course of that inquiry.

In that year, in my view, the menace of gunmen in London was as great, if not greater, than it is today. A number of gangs had formed, and many carried guns which experience in the Forces had taught them to use. And they did not hesitate to do so.

It was due in no small measure to the brilliant team work of these three fearless officers that that menace at that time was defeated. I worked in close contact with these officers at that time, and know, how through the finding of a mackintosh which one of the gunmen had discarded the three gunmen were traced, captured and convicted. Two of them were hanged; the third was too young.

Immediately afterwards there was a giant combined effort by Yard officers, and a large number of men found carrying guns were rounded up. Messages were sent to every area chief, and to senior officers in all the Home Counties where there had been hold-ups, to view these men, and see whether they answered the descriptions of men who had committed gun hold-ups in their area.

It brought satisfactory results, and later police found abandoned guns all over the place—in parks, empty houses, and from the Thames. The gangsters were clearly shown that carrying a gun did not pay. In the following year the Commissioner was able to report a marked decrease in armed robberies.

Fabian retired from the police force in 1949 after 28 years distinguished service. He joined as a police-constable on the beat, and like so many of his colleagues whose names became household words in the great Metropolis, graduated from a police-constable on the beat, to an *aide*, and then full-time detective work.

Great detectives like Chief-Superintendents Steven Glander, Bert Sparks (the Iron Man,) Bob Stone, Bert Griffin, and Ted Greeno all rose from the ranks as did Commander George

Hatherill, the former head of detectives, and his deputy now Commander Ernest Millen. So did the late Commander Reginald Spooner and Chief-Superintendents Nat Thorp, Tom Barrett and Bill Chapman.

Their places are being taken by men of no less ability, and from the higher ranks to the present-day police-constable on the beat, of no less courage and endurance in the battle against villains. Men still ready and fully prepared to hazard their health and their lives in safeguarding the lives and property of others.

Men for example like Police-Constable William Couzens who joined the force in 1957 and was stationed at Tottenham Court Road police station, headquarters of the de Antiquis murder hunt. He's had dealings with a gunman, too. In September 1963, he and two other officers were patrolling in a police car in the West End when they saw four men acting suspiciously.

They decided to find out what these men were up to, but as the officers approached one bolted. No innocent man bolts in such circumstances so P.C. Couzens hared after him. Suddenly the man turned, brandished a pistol and yelled, "Go away."

P.C. Couzens drew his truncheon, and as he did so he heard a click as the man pulled the trigger. He did not hesitate. He jumped at the man and forced the gun from his hand as he overpowered him. Later he learned that the gun had three live rounds in the magazine, but it could not be fired because the firing pin was missing. But the officer did not know this—and neither did the gunman! In April 1964, P.C. Couzens was awarded the Queen's Commendation for brave conduct.

Detective-Inspector Robert Huntley and P.C. John Russell went to a gaming club in Fulham in October 1963, when they received a report that an armed man had just shot at the proprietor. They knew the man they were going to tackle, known in the Underworld as "Mad Ronnie" had a loaded pistol, but neither sought a gun.

They walked boldly into the club, tackled the man, and

after a brief struggle, overpowered him. They found live rounds in the gun when they examined it, and, for their action both were awarded the British Empire Medal for gallantry in May 1963.

Often the most simple incident leads to violence, and too often the police are the victims. Police-Constable Robert Hirons, aged 24, was patrolling on a lightweight motor-cycle in Brixton one day not long ago when he saw three coloured men interfering with parked cars. When he approached all three attacked him, knocked him down and kicked him.

A detective arrived and rushed to the constable's help. He arrested one man, and the other two ran away. Despite his injuries P.C. Hirons gave chase and caught up with them. Once again he was attacked and the men escaped, but, fortunately, they were caught later and P.C. Hirons was commended at the Old Bailey and by the Commissioner for his "courage and persistence."

P.C. Graham Carpenter served for two years as a Police-Cadet before he became a P.C., and his first brush with villains came when he was only 19. He was patrolling a beat in Kilburn when he saw two men carrying bulky packages climb from the first floor window of a shop.

It was 5 a.m., and when they saw the young officer they bolted. P.C. Carpenter chased after them and caught one man. During the struggle that followed the second man ran to a car and drove it on to the pavement trying to run down the policeman. He missed, tried again, and again failed. Then a patrol car arrived, both men were captured, and sent to prison. P.C. Carpenter was commended by the Commissioner for his "courage and tenacity."

Men like these, men like P.C. David Lusty, are always ready for the unexpected. P.C. Lusty was one of a patrol car crew called to a reservoir in Surrey when the driver of a dumper reversed his vehicle too far, and went into the water with it. P.C. Lusty immediately stripped off his uniform and dived in.

He dived several times before he located the dumper with the driver trapped by his legs under the machine about ten

feet down. He tried in vain to free the man, so he secured a
rope, and then assisted in raising the dumper by means of a
mobile digging machine, so that the driver could be freed. He
brought the man to the surface but, unfortunately, all attempts
at artificial respiration failed. P.C. Lusty received the Commissioner's commendation for "courage and perseverance."

These officers, and their colleagues on the beat and in patrol
cars at this very moment are the Fabian's and the senior officers
of tomorrow. Call them at any time of the day and night and
they will be at your service. No job is too big for them. No
criminal too tough to handle.

You may call our policemen any names you like. There
is one thing you cannot call them. You cannot call them
cowards.

INDEX

With ranks at time of incident.